4/94

Department of the Environment

Evaluation of Urban Development Grant, Urban Regeneration Grant and City Grant

Price Waterhouse

LONDON: HMSO

75891 7/2W

Contents

Executive Summary

INTRODUCTION

1 This is the final report in a study commissioned by the Department of the Environment (DOE) to evaluate the impact of City Grant and its predecessors (Urban Regeneration Grant and Urban Development Grant). Hereafter, we refer to the various regimes as City Grant for simplicity. An interim report was presented following the completion of stage 1 which analysed twenty projects. Stage 2, analysing a further 16 projects has subsequently been completed. This report discusses the combined results of the work carried out in stages 1 and 2.

2 The evaluation has addressed the following objectives:

- Evaluation of the success of the grant aided projects in contributing to the wider regeneration of the local area,
- Evaluation of the success of individual grant aided projects in meeting their stated objectives,
- Identification of success factors associated with the achievements (or otherwise) of the objectives,
- Recommendations for future policy formulation.

3 The objective of City Grant is to assist private sector development projects in the 57 inner city areas which would otherwise be unable to proceed because project costs exceed completed development value.

4 Throughout the evaluation we have been keen to measure only those impacts which can genuinely be associated with the City Grant assistance given to a project. In doing so we have followed the DoE guidelines to determine net additionality for each project. In particular we have assessed each project in terms of:

- property market impact,
- economic impact,
- environmental impact,
- social and community impact,
- value for money.

We will briefly discuss each of these in turn.

THE PROPERTY MARKET IMPACT

5 The impact of City Grant on the property market has been considered in relation to:

- the generation of net additional property investment which would not otherwise have occurred in the area,
- indirect effects such as:
  - induced property development in neighbouring areas,
  - effects of grant aided schemes on land values.

6 We have tried to avoid second guessing the original appraisal, but we believe that, in all the projects considered grant aid enabled a development to take place which would otherwise not have occurred in the short to medium term.

7 With reference to induced demand, there are a number of instances where we believe that a grant aided scheme has had the effect of encouraging other developers to enter the local market as a hidden demand is revealed.

8 The impact of City Grant on land values is difficult to assess. In the case of eligible land values in City Grant applications the DOE restrict this to the alternative use value in a no grant world. The impact on surrounding land is, however, more difficult to assess and increases in land value can have detrimental as well as beneficial effects.

9 Our research indicated that although developers, local authorities, agents etc said that individual projects had no impact on land values, the effect of City Grant in combination with other initiatives has, over time, led to increased confidence in the area and ultimately to higher land values.

10 This may not be a bad thing as it shows grant aided projects are contributing to the creation of a viable development market which previously had not existed. Difficulties arise when grant aided schemes lead surrounding landowners to perceive (hope value) that their sites are worth more than their market value. In such cases landowners will not sell their sites unless they receive what is perceived to be the value of their site. In many cases, the holding costs of inner city land to companies is low in absolute terms, there is no need to sell unless their

perceived value is achieved. This can in turn lead to regeneration being prevented.

ECONOMIC IMPACT

11 We have estimated economic impact by considering job creation. There are, of course, other forms of economic impact including wealth/income creation, increased output, fostering of trading links etc. However, in line with the DoE methodology, we have used **net additional job creation** as a convenient proxy for these other impacts.

12 In determining the level of job creation which can be directly attributable to the City Grant it is necessary to take account of:

- those jobs which would have happened in any case in the absence of the scheme (deadweight),
- those jobs which have merely been transferred from other locations (displacement).

13 By taking account of deadweight and displacement we are able to work back to a figure which we think can be genuinely attributable to the City Grant.

14 At the time of the appraisals, the target set was to create 6,271 full time equivalent jobs. In the schemes sampled, 5,271 Full time equivalent (FTE) jobs were created, some 19% below the figure predicted.

15 None of these jobs were considered to be deadweight but 46% (2,416 jobs) were displaced from other premises in the area, leaving a figure of 2,855 net additional jobs which could be said to have resulted from the City Grant. This is just under half the estimate at the time of appraisal. It should be noted however that although the DOE's approach to forecasting jobs prior to the project going ahead makes insufficient allowance for displacement they advised us that their approach compensates for this by setting low cost per job guidelines, and that it takes no account of construction jobs or off site multipler effects.

16 We also looked at other indicators of economic performance, in particular, supply linkages. Backward supply linkages in the local economy (level of purchases) give a good indication of indirect job creation. Office and Industrial schemes provided the highest level of purchases within the inner area, followed by Hotels, with Retail schemes being the lowest. The low level of purchases by Retail operations and Hotels can in part be attributed to many of them being part of national multiples with centralised purchasing and distribution.

17 The number of employees in assisted schemes who are resident in the inner area was analysed, in order to assess the potential increase in the income of the inner area population; an indication of the level of local income multipliers. Retail and Hotel projects employed the highest proportion of employees from within the inner area (53% and 46% respectively) followed by Industrial schemes at 32% and Offices at 21%.

ENVIRONMENTAL IMPACT

18 In analysing environmental impact, we devised some quantifiable indicators and explored other, more qualitative, measures of environmental impact. We assessed environmental impact on the site itself and at the wider local area.

19 In considering the environmental impacts at the site level we looked at a number of factors including:

- visibility,
- removal of dereliction,
- quality of design.

20 When analysing the local area (within 0.5 km of the scheme boundary) we looked at, among others:

- traffic/parking,
- pollution.

21 In general all the projects in the sample contributed to an improvement in their respective sites and local areas. Prominent or vacant sites improved the environment most significantly and most projects contributed to other public sector initiatives and investment programmes.

22 We noted that environmental improvements were often not specifically referred to in the appraisal papers, but consider that the impact of environmental improvement in encouraging urban regeneration should not be underestimated. We do however recognise that the majority of the schemes we looked at are several years old and many have now been completed. The case papers have therefore evolved over time and the current papers do take more account of the importance of environmental improvement. Economic regeneration (including property development) is heavily reliant on confidence, and physical signs of improvement play an important role in encouraging investment decisions. Whilst this is difficult to measure and convert into direct and immediate benefits it can nevertheless offer a significant contribution to longer term economic development momentum. Environmental improvements are among the most important impacts of City Grant.

SOCIAL AND COMMUNITY IMPACT

23 Social and community impacts were not given the same emphasis when City Grant was introduced as they had been under Urban Development Grant. Indeed the 1988 guidance notes omitted any reference to these impacts. The 1992 revised guidance notes do however refer to

> "an increase in the choice of facilities available in the area"

24 Social and community impacts are important both in their own right, and for economic development. The removal of hazards and visual blight improves local self esteem and confidence. Improvements in job opportunities for local residents reduce levels of deprivation, and provide local economic growth through expenditure on consumption.

25 Despite the fact that appraisers rarely referred to social and community benefits (the appraisal process did not set 'social' targets) we identified some considerable social and community benefits arising from City Grant schemes.

In particular:

- housing schemes provided a greater choice for local residents in terms of cost and tenure arrangements
- retail schemes provided additional social activity and meeting points
- schemes incorporating visual improvement did much to enhance local civic pride and social self esteem.

VALUE FOR MONEY

26 We assessed value for money in terms of grant effectiveness (gross and net outputs) and efficiency (ratio of inputs to outputs) for each project in the sample.

Turning to effectiveness, job creation by each broad floorspace use type is given below:

Table 1 – Outputs: Net additional job creation

Use Type	Gross Job Creation	Net Additional Job Creation	% Net Additional
Offices	1,490	422	28%
Industrial	1,889	1,012	54%
Retail	1,203	809	67%
Hotels	689	612	89%
TOTAL	5271	2855	54%

27 A comparison of outputs shows that (third column) hotels were most efficient in generating net additional jobs although when comparing these outputs with inputs, the table below shows that the cost per hotel job was significantly higher than in other schemes.

Table 2 – Net public sector cost per net additional job achieved

Use Type	1991 Cost Per Net Addition Job
	£
Offices	13,696
Industrial	12,358
Retail	14,319
Hotels	17,810
TOTAL	14,280

Table 3 – Net Public Expenditure as a proportion of Net Private Investment (Gearing ratio)

Use Type	Public Expenditure As A Proportion Of Private Investment	
Offices	1:6.8	15%
Industrial	1:4.0	25%
Retail	1:7.0	14%
Hotels	1:2.8	35%
OVERALL	1:5	20%

28 In general these cost per job and gearing figures reveal that, in terms of value for money, City Grant compared relatively favourably with other public sector job creation initiatives.

POLICY CONCLUSIONS

29 Our policy recommendations conclude that City Grant is a successful policy instrument although there is scope for evolutionary improvements in the future. In particular, a wider range of policy mechanisms are needed (in part to enable follow through policies).

30 City Grant as a policy has a relatively narrow range of objectives which could be specified more fully to enable a more precise policy evaluation. We also believe that the range of objectives could be enlarged to:

- encompass those factors which are responsible for sustained economic growth;
- specify more precisely any environmental, social and community objectives which policy makers consider that the grant should achieve.

1 Introduction

STUDY OBJECTIVES

31 Price Waterhouse was commissioned by the Department of the Environment to evaluate the impact of Urban Development Grant, Urban Regeneration Grant and City Grant. The study was undertaken in two phases and this report has been prepared after the completion of both.

32 The objectives of the study were:

- To evaluate a sample of grant aided projects to seen how successful they were in meeting the objectives of the programmes.
- To assess the success of the sampled projects in contributing to the wider regeneration of their local area.
- To identify the factors associated with the achievement of the project and programme objectives and regenerative impact.
- To make recommendations for refinements to the existing City Grant programme, in terms of the criteria used in appraisal and the overall shape of the programme, to ensure that the programme produces the most significant regenerative effects in the future.

33 These objectives were amended to include the following issues at Phase 2.

- The extent to which grant aided schemes induced development in neighbouring areas;
- Whether there is evidence of displacement in the property market arising from grant aided projects;
- The impact of grants on job creation;
- The effect of grant on land values.

34 The study did not aim to evaluate the impact of the programme as a whole; nor were we concerned with the way in which the programme is operated. These aspects were both covered in an earlier study of Urban Development Grant by Aston University.

THE AIMS OF CITY GRANT

35 City Grant and its predecessors is given to major private sector capital schemes which would otherwise be unable to proceed because, as a result of their inner city sites and locations, costs exceed values. Priority is given to projects in the 57 designated urban programme areas. Within these, projects are generally located within the inner areas.

36 The aims of City Grant and its predecessors are "to promote the economic and physical regeneration of inner urban areas by levering private sector investment into such areas". UDG projects were also expected to "make a demonstrable contribution to meeting the special social needs of inner urban areas and creating a climate of confidence for the private sector".

37 A wide range of types of project are eligible, including industrial, commercial and leisure, and housing. The benefits provided by schemes may be in the form of jobs, private housing or other facilities.

38 Whereas applications for UDG had to be submitted through a Local Authority, and some local authorities played a highly proactive role in encouraging development of particular kinds in specific locations, the role of the public sector in City Grant is much more reactive in that there is no longer any direct local authority involvement and it is therefore much more private sector driven. This is important to remember when evaluating the degree to which the objectives of the regime are met.

APPROACH TO THE RESEARCH

39 The first phase of the study started in June 1990 and an interim report was submitted in April 1991. The second phase was commenced in October 1991 and completed in July 1992. This report contains our findings and conclusions, based on both phases.

The sample

40 The study has involved an in-depth examination of 36 selected grant-aided projects. Twenty-one projects were examined in Phase 1 of the study, and a further fifteen in Phase 2.

41 To make the most effective use of resources and to help us to disentangle the effects of scheme

characteristics from those of local property market conditions, the first phase projects were chosen from within five conurbations: Birmingham, South Tyneside, Nottingham, Oldham and Hull. These cities were chosen because they each contained a significant number of projects with a wide range of characteristics which could have had a knock-on effect on each other.

42   The samples were carefully selected to be broadly representative of the population of grant-aided projects, but were not intended to be statistically representative. The reader should therefore be cautious in assuming that the results of this analysis would apply across the programme as a whole.

43   The sample for Phase 2 was chosen to contain as many completed City Grant projects as were available at the time.

44   The projects were chosen to illustrate a variety of features:

   - Different types of use
   - Large and small schemes
   - Size of grant awarded
   - New build and refurbishment
   - Different locational characteristics
   - Isolated and clustered grant-aided schemes
   - Property developments and business developments.

Data sources

45   For each project, our research included:

   - A study of the Department's case papers
   - An interview with the developer
   - A survey of the occupants of the scheme
   - Interviews with the local authority
   - Discussions with local property agents
   - Site visits
   - Interviews with officers of the Department of the Environment
   - Consultation with local community representatives
   - Collection of background data on the local economy and property market.

Developer Interviews

46   Interviews with developers were used to collect factual information on the developer and the project itself, and to obtain the developer's views on such issues as the impact of the availability of grant on his actions, and his perception of the risks and rewards of inner city development.

47   Interviews were concluded with all but one developer. Henry Boot the developer of Paradise Circus in Birmingham refused to cooperate as they maintained that the grant was in fact given to the City Council (for their car park) and to the hotel operator, and that their involvement was simply as a contractor. For that reason they saw no value in discussing the development.

48   The quality of information obtained from the developer interviews varied across the sample. This was due to the varying ability of interviewees to recall objectively the circumstances surrounding a grant application made several years ago, especially when there was a requirement to recall dates, costs and values.

49   Also within the development companies numerous personnel changes have occurred since the respective grant applications.

Occupiers

50   For Phase 1 of the study telephone interviews were carried out with 50 of the 85 identified occupiers – a completion rate of 59%. Phase 2 data was collected from a postal survey of 169 occupants with a total of 91 questionnaires completed and returned, representing a 53% return rate. Thus the return rate for the entire sample was 55%. Occupants were asked about their premises, employees and business.

Local authorities

51   Discussions were held with officers in local authority economic development and planning departments and any other departments able to provide information on the scheme or the surrounding area. The purpose of these discussions was to obtain information about the background to the scheme, how scheme objectives related to the local property market, and perceptions about changes in the area around the scheme.

Local property agents and property market data

52   We talked to local property agents to obtain their views on the impact the schemes have had in generating confidence and inducing further investment in the area. We also reviewed any analyses prepared by them on trends in the local property market.

53   Our interviews were supplemented by published data on available floorspace and rentals in the different market segments.

Site visits

54   All the sites were visited by at least one member of the team to collect information with which to assess environmental impact and obtain an impression of current conditions in the neighbourhood.

Department of the Environment

55   We talked to the leader of the appraisal team and others within the City Grant Division in central and regional office.

Success indicators

56   The impact of individual projects was assessed in relation to the following indicators:

- Property market impact: property market displacement, induced investment and impact on land values
- Economic impact: employment creation
- Environmental impact: project quality, visual impact, removal of dereliction
- Value for money: additionality, grant per unit of output, gearing.
- Social and community benefits: housing, jobs, facilities for local residents.

57   This report contains our final findings and conclusions for both phases of the review. It draws on the information and tentative conclusions reached in Phase 1 of our study. It provides firm conclusions based on the sample and includes a number of policy recommendations for consideration by the Department. This report also supersedes the initial report submitted in April 1991.

REPORT STRUCTURE

58   The remainder of this report has the following structure:

- Chapter 2 – The Property Market Impact.
- Chapter 3 – Economic Impact.
- Chapter 4 – Environmental Impact.
- Chapter 5 – Social and Community Impact.
- Chapter 6 – Value For Money.
- Chapter 7 – Policy Conclusions.

2 Property Market Impact

INTRODUCTION

59 This chapter examines the extent to which grant aid generated additional private sector investment in the inner area and the wider impact this had on the local property market. In particular we have set out to examine three key effects.

- Additionality of Investment.
- Induced Investment.
- The Impact on Land Values.

60 Prior to considering these issues in detail we have set the context of the chapter by briefly discussing the following:

- Data Sources.
- External Economic Factors.
- The Property Cycle.

Data Sources

61 Property market impact has been assessed using data from the following sources:

- Interviews with the developer of each project.
- Interviews with local authorities.
- Statistics prepared by local authorities.
- Interviews with local property agents.
- Statistics prepared by property agents.
- Interviews with members of the City Grant appraisal team, and the head of the City Grant Division.
- Occupier Survey.
- Interviews with a limited number of developers responsible for projects in the vicinity of a grant-aided project.

62 Interviews with developers were used to collect factual information on the project, to obtain views on such issues as the impact of the availability of grant on their actions and to assess perceptions of the risks and rewards of inner city development.

63 Local Authorities and agents were a valuable source of views and statistics on wider trends in the property market, and the impact of the grant-aided projects in stimulating neighbourhood regeneration.

64 The assistance of appraisers and administrators within City Grant Division has been particularly important as a means of reconciling and moderating conflicting feedback, especially where key personalities in development companies had moved on and it was necessary to counter post hoc rationalisations of courses of action given by people who were not there at the time.

External Economic Factors

65 It was recognised at the time when the study was commissioned that it would be difficult to disaggregate the effect of the grant regime on the property market from the more general economic trends. From 1983, the date of the first Urban Development Grant submission, through to the present date has seen a period where business confidence was initially low, grew rapidly, and then declined again.

66 These changes had a particular impact upon the *cost* and the *supply* of money for property development, and thus affected key variables determining the price and nature of development.

- Cost: At the outset of the period, inflation was high, and business confidence low. This had the effect of raising the level of returns required from development, and reducing values. Later, confidence improved and inflation fell, until 1989, when interest rates rose again before falling again in the early 1990's. By 1992 interest rates had fallen considerably, although still high in real terms. Small changes in long term interest rates have a profound effect on the viability of property development – far greater than any effects directly attributable to site specific factors.
- Supply: The liberalisation of capital markets has meant that compared with 1983, when the first UDG awards were made, there is a far greater supply of both capital and providers of capital available to property developers. Although the cost of finance is also a factor, it was possible in the late 1980's early 1990's to borrow money on short and medium terms which would have been simply unobtainable in 1983. The current recession has, however,

reduced the financial institutions willingness to support property development schemes. Again, supply of capital is a general condition, which is not site-specific.

67 To a great extent, the appraisal process took due regard of these external factors, and made every effort to reflect the realities of market conditions applying at the time. However, two factors combined to reduce the sensitivity of the appraisal to up to date market intelligence. These were:

- The appraisal process, particularly of early applications, frequently took a great deal of time. (The introduction of City Grant and the setting of targets for timing of processing application has substantially improved this.) Market evidence suggests that changes in value, and perceptions about the growth potential of a site or a location, often took place very rapidly, perhaps triggered by a single deal which demonstrated the feasibility of doing things which, previously, developers would have thought too risky.
- Developers themselves, having received an offer of grant, often took time over negotiating an appropriate agreement with the local authority (in the case of UDG) or the Department (in case of City Grant) or indeed implementing the proposals. In other cases, the local authority side was slow. In a rising market this could give an unintended bonus to the developer.

68 Economic conditions improved so rapidly in the mid to late 1980's that, with the benefit of hindsight, it is clear that the risks of implementing projects were frequently much less than anticipated at appraisal. This does however appear to reflect the market at that time and we found no evidence to suggest developers used delay as a deliberate tactic to reduce risk.

The Property Cycle

69 The analysis of grant aided schemes needs to take account of the cyclical nature of the property market at both a national and local level. After reaching a peak at the start of 1979, year on year growth in total property returns went into decline and by mid-1982, property was showing nil growth. From that time, however, a sustained recovery in demand was experienced in all sectors of the economy to be followed, in varying degrees, by recovery in property development activity. Total property returns, however, lingered at or below 10% for the next five years as the over-supply in accommodation halted any significant escalation in rental performance. By 1987, rental performance had begun to improve as the late 1980's property boom

continued to gather momentum. This was fuelled by a rare combination of events, namely:

- A depressed equity market following the Stock Market collapse in October 1987 which encouraged institutions towards property investments.
- A shortage of supply and an increasing demand for most types of property.
- The increased availability and low cost of finance.
- A liberalisation of planning legislation allowing increased development activity.
- Increases in disposable income arising from tax reductions and a sharp rise in property owners equity, especially in the South East.

70 It was becoming increasingly evident by 1989 that a chronic over-supply was imminent in certain sectors of the property market. Interest rates peaked at 15% in October 1989 and by early 1990, the signals of a strong cyclical downturn were self evident.

71 The property development cycle does not, however, occur uniformly throughout the United Kingdom nor is it uniform between sectors of the property industry. In 1988 retail properties experienced rental growth of 23% with industrial properties showing growth of 25%. Within the City of London, the office boom commenced in mid-1986 to be followed in 1987 by a similar boom in office development in London's West End. By 1988 it had reached the United Kingdom's major provincial office centres and in that year office rentals rose by an average of 28%. In Newcastle between 1986 and 1989 rents rose from £4.50 psf to £8.50 psf and in Leicester, over the same period, prime rents rose from the same base level to almost £10 psf.

72 In contrast to the office boom, the retail boom first affected the "North". By the late 1980s, the ripple effect had acted in reverse with major retail development activity occurring in the "South".

73 It is clear that rapidly escalating rental levels, stable property yields and development periods often well in excess of twelve months, made project appraisal a difficult process. In retrospect, the risk attached to a number of schemes on completion was undeniably much less than originally predicted. However, by contrast, some schemes undertaken towards the end of the 1980s have arguably hit their respective markets at the "wrong" time with outturn risk being considerably higher than that anticipated.

74 Figure 2.1 provides a graph comparing property returns with interest rates for the period 1981–1992. In Figure 2.2 the durations of our sample schemes, on a sectoral basis, has been plotted. By considering these together a simplistic assessment of each schemes appearance on the market in relation to the

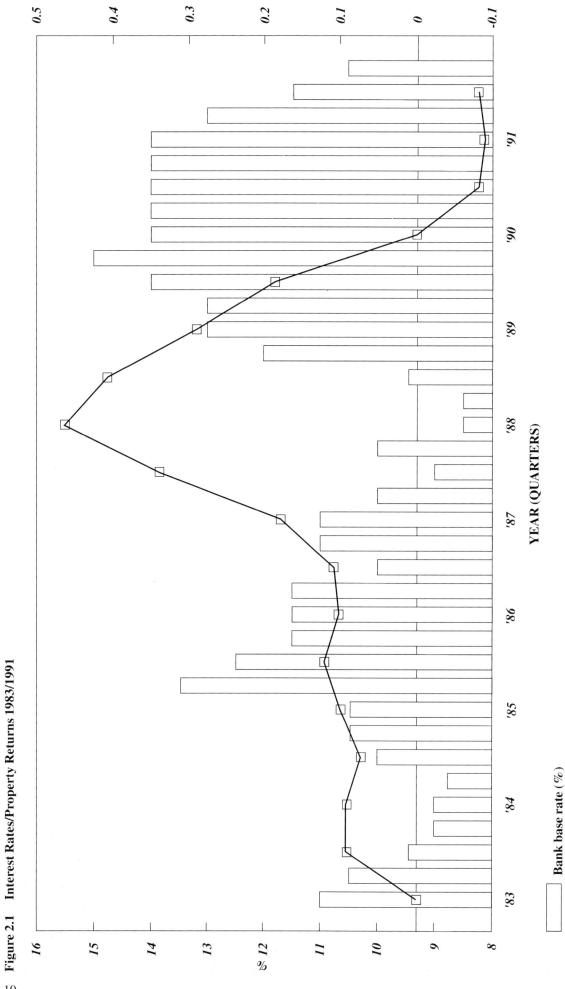

Figure 2.1   Interest Rates/Property Returns 1983/1991

Sources;   Bank base rate: Bank of England
Total property return index: Investors Chronicle/Hillier Parker

Bank base rate (%)

Total property return index (year-on-year growth)

Year-on-Year Growth

YEAR (QUARTERS)

Figure 2.2 SCHEME DURATION DATES

YEAR (QUARTERS)

	1983	1984	1985	1986	1987	1988	1989	1990	1991
	1 2 3 4	1 2 3 4	1 2 3 4	1 2 3 4	1 2 3 4	1 2 3 4	1 2 3 4	1 2 3 4	1 2 3 4

Offices

- Birmingham, 3–5 St Paul's Square
- Oldham, Union Street
- Birmingham, Snowhill Station
- Nottingham, Stoney Street
- Manchester, Newcastle House
- Manchester, Albion House
- Newcastle, 43–49 Grey Street
- Leicester, Arnhem House
- Sheffield, Huttons Buildings
- Southwark, Archbishop Temple Units

Industrial

- Birmingham, IMI Holford Park
- Birmingham, Newhall Hill
- Oldham, Stamford Mill
- Oldham, MCM Ltd
- Nottingham, Southglade Park
- Nottingham, Beechdale Engineering
- Birmingham, Garrison Lane
- Birmingham, Startpoint Industrial Units
- Boldon, Boldon Business Park
- Hartlepool, Hartlepool Business Park
- Southwark, Priter Way Arches

Retail

- Bolton, Bark Street
- South Shields, Catherine Street
- Hull, Bransholme North
- Gateshead, Felling Town Centre
- Middlesbrough, Zetland Road
- Birmingham, One Stop, Perry Bar

Hotels

- Birmingham, Paradise Circus
- Manchester, Midland Hotel
- Nottingham, Rutland Square Hotel

Housing

- Hull, Courtauld's Warehouse
- Hull, Coltman Street
- Birmingham, The Parade
- Nottingham, Southglade Park
- Nottingham, Mundella Court
- Oldham, Bank Top Mill

SCHEME START DATE – Date Grant Awarded
SCHEME COMPLETION DATE – Provided by Developer

property development cycle can be assessed and this helps to explain why certain projects were more successful than others.

75 Clearly the impact of City Grant on the local property market cannot be looked at in isolation and it is recognised that disentangling this from other external factors is fraught with difficulty. We have, however, in the following sections analysed the project sample to consider the extent to which investment in the local property market was additional, whether this investment induced further development and the impact of grant aided projects on land values.

ADDITIONALITY OF INVESTMENT

76 Additionality is the extent to which the payment of grant resulted in development that would not otherwise have occurred, would have occurred much later or in a substantially curtailed form, or which displaces other investment. In assessing whether the investment was additional we determined the gross additional investment and subtracted deadweight and displacement.

Deadweight

77 Deadweight is investment that would have occurred in the absence of grant aid either because the project did not need the aid to progress or it would have received sufficient other aid instead.

78 In all but one case the developers maintained that they would not have proceeded without grant. The exception was Grey Street, Newcastle where the appraised rent was £6–8 psf although £13.50 psf was achieved on completion. With hindsight this shows the grant was not needed. This does not, however, undermine the appraiser's conclusions that the applicant would not have proceeded at the time he did unless offered grant. The subsequent rise in value would eventually have induced the developer to proceed unaided and in fact this rise eventually led to the recovery of approximately 50% of the grant via the clawback mechanism.

79 Although this was the only project where the developer stated he would have proceeded without grant, there were some projects which benefitted from the rapid growth in property values in the late 1980's and which, with benefit of hindsight, could have been undertaken without grant aid. This viability is measured by the extent to which "clawback" was payable to the DoE and is analysed in detail in Chapter 6.

80 Although this suggests, that grant aid in these circumstances did not generate additional investment

and that it simply brought it forward in time, this does assume that;

- The market gap at which the project was aimed would have stayed open.
- The developer would have been able, willing and prepared to undertake the scheme at a later date.

If neither of these are certain we consider investment should be classed as gross additional.

Displacement

81 To ascertain whether the investment is a net addition we also need to consider displacement effects. This occurs when the generation of a desirable programme output leads to the loss of the same output elsewhere. This may occur where there are resource constraints or where demand is constrained so an assisted project wins market share at the expense of competitors.

82 Property market displacement occurs where either:

- A developer substitutes a grant aided project for another non-grant aided project.
- Projects by other developers are not undertaken as a result of a grant aided project being carried out or existing businesses are damaged.

83 Developer substitution may occur if there are constraints on inputs such as finance or expertise. It may be direct where a developer faced with the choice between a grant aided and non-grant aided scheme opts for the former, or indirect where because of resource constraints a developer can only carry out one scheme and a grant aided scheme is being undertaken in favour of an as yet unknown alternative.

84 In our sample there was no evidence that investment was being directly diverted and in many cases even indirect substitution appears unlikely. Few developers had alternative schemes available and although it is true that if one project proves abortive the capital will eventually be invested elsewhere this will involve a time lag and the alternative project may not necessarily be a property development in the inner city.

85 The characteristics of the developers also suggests that substitution is unlikely. The majority are either small development companies who have previously only undertaken a limited number of projects e.g. Crofton Place Estate Company Limited, (Hutton Buildings, Sheffield); or companies specifically established by larger parent companies to act as development companies e.g. English & Overseas Properties, (Startpoint Industrial Units,

Birmingham). In either case such companies are unlikely to be considering a range of development opportunities and therefore the substitution impact is unlikely to be high.

86   In the strictest sense, displacement refers to a situation where public assistance allows output (in this case commercial and residential property) to be put on the market which could compete with existing supply.

87   A potential failing in public sector inspired schemes in the past has been that they have either added floorspace in a market which was already oversupplied or they have artificially kept down the rental/capital value of schemes and thereby crowded out the private sector. This attitude was prominent in the 1970's and early 1980's in areas like North East England where industrial supply was dominated by English Estates, and Scotland where the Scottish Development Agency was also a major provider of industrial floorspace. It might have been expected, therefore, that schemes assisted by UDG or City Grant would have attracted the same criticism. In point of fact we found no evidence to suggest that either displacement or crowding out has occurred.

88   It is however important to draw a distinction in terms of quality of product, to avoid coming to the false conclusion that new floorspace must create displacement if it is added to a market that is technically oversupplied. In several inner areas we visited, particular property sectors were subject to technical oversupply at the time the project began, often as a result of over-active development in previous boom periods. Often, however, the quality of this vacant space was too low for it to be considered an effective part of the stock.

89   Our analysis revealed that the majority of occupants considered that the grant aided scheme met a demand that was not being supplied by other vacant property in the market. Furthermore, occupiers stated that they were paying at least the market rate for the accommodation in that location and that cheaper premises which were in some cases available were simply unacceptable.

90   In considering displacement in its widest sense, it is necessary to look beyond quantitative factors alone and to examine the extent to which the product is new to the market; that is, the extent to which a project could be described as pioneering. This may relate to property sectors (for example, the first hotel development), quality or even tenure.

91   Below, we summarise our analysis of some specific projects in terms of displacement.

92   **Union Street, Oldham**: This scheme represented a mere 2.25% of the total office stock within the local authority area although it provided almost all of the quality accommodation in the town. The development was a pioneer in an extremely weak market for office accommodation and further development only occurred when the scheme had been fully let and sold. The project did not, therefore, displace other office development and indeed, may have actually induced further investment.

93   **Arnhem House, Leicester**: In Leicester, it was known in the market-place prior to the development by London & Manchester Assurance of Arnhem House that the eventual occupier, Royal Insurance, was seeking to rationalise its accommodation within the city. Despite the abundance of office accommodation particularly around the Inner Ring Road, it was not considered likely that Royal Insurance would relocate from its various offices within the city to a low quality, secondhand 1960's or 1970's block. The accountants, KPMG Peat Marwick, had already set a new tone by occupying a prominent and very striking grant-aided development on a site adjacent to that developed by London & Manchester Assurance. Arnhem House did not, therefore, displace existing office space but created a new product for which a demand existed.

94   **Snowhill & Paradise Circus, Birmingham**: In Birmingham the developments at Snowhill Station and Paradise Circus added to the stock of office accommodation at a time when there was technically 500,000 sq ft of good quality space known to be available for occupation. The Snowhill Station development achieved the highest rent for Birmingham in early 1985, a rent which was not exceeded until early 1988 when supply and demand conditions had tightened. However, there is no evidence that Ernst & Young, who occupied Phase 1 of the Snowhill Station scheme, could have found a developer to provide another building, of equal quality in a suitable location, unless that developer had also received UDG. Whilst other existing property was perhaps available, it was again not considered suitable due to either quality, location or unit size, even though the rent might have been lower.

95   **Newcastle House & Stoney Street, Nottingham**: These two developments in Nottingham both occurred at a point when the vacancy level in the city for post war office accommodation was rising. At the time when the Stoney Street grant was awarded, the City Council stated that some 190,000 sq ft of post war office space was vacant, representing 12.7% of total stock. Indeed proposals for office development in Nottingham were, by early 1988, dominated by grant aided developments (310,000 sq ft) whilst private sector development without grant was limited to small scale office refurbishments (and totalled only 179,750 sq ft).

Similar conditions of high vacancy levels existed in the Birmingham industrial market prior to and immediately following the decision taken by IMI Metals Plc to develop at Holford Park. In all these cases it is clear that the existing supply of accommodation was not what the market was demanding and the grant aided schemes by providing this could not be accused of displacing existing floorspace.

96   **Garrison Lane, Birmingham**: Tenure is another issue that can potentially lead to an otherwise normal building appealing to a particular target market. The industrial development at Garrison Lane, in Birmingham was, on the face of it, nothing new to the market. It did, however, offer prospective occupiers the opportunity to acquire premises outright by disposal of freehold titles and therefore filled a market niche that was not being met. Again we do not consider that this implies displacement.

97   Our interviews with the developers of the Phase II projects, revealed additional evidence that grant-aided schemes had little or no negative impact on other developer intentions in the area. Twelve out of fifteen developers contended that their project had no adverse impact on competing developments. The remaining three actually considered there to be positive links, i.e. induced development was believed to have occurred. While the actual developers opinions are perhaps not surprising, our more limited interviews with developers of non-grant aided schemes concurred with these views.

98   The analysis of housing schemes is much more difficult in terms of impact on existing stock and any displacement effects. Housing is the most segmented of any of the property markets and demand is dominated by households transferring between segments over their life cycle.

99   Ultimately any addition to stock accelerates the process of replacement and the improvement of space and amenity standards. The developments that provide the highest benefits are those which increase the range on offer to the market and in turn increase its efficiency by allowing free movement between type, location and tenure.

100   Housing schemes like The Parade in Birmingham, Courtauld's Warehouse in Hull and Bank Top Mill in Oldham all demonstrate how accommodation of a particular type, price brand and tenure can prove to be extremely popular although the market ordinarily would not have provided such a product at that time. In the case of the former two developments, they involved the creation of accommodation by an applicant whose main business was not property development. These companies were not bound by the development inertia in providing "more of the same" to established market segments whose needs

and market comparables were easily identifiable. In the case of Bank Top Mill the developer was targeting a market that had previously been viewed as being satisfied by the large stock of low-priced Victorian terraced housing stock.

101   All three developments met a particular market need which had previously neither been identified or perceived as necessary.

Conclusion

102   Not surprisingly, displacement will tend to be lower where grant helps to make viable a development of a unique quality and either creates a new market segment or supplements an existing segment which is suffering from undersupply. Developments bringing forward "more of the same" to a market either in equilibrium or facing technical oversupply tend to show relatively higher levels of displacement. On balance we considered that the majority of the grant aided projects were net additional. Only one project, Grey Street, Newcastle, was classified as deadweight and there were only limited signs of displacement occurring in the property market.

INDUCED INVESTMENT

103   The converse of market displacement is induced investment, where grant aided development leads the way to creating a market which previously did not exist in a locality and therefore triggers further development. The demonstration effect is central to the rationale of creating induced investment, although there are inherent difficulties in isolating the impact of an individual project. In assessing this we have considered projects from our sample within the context of three external factors.

● The timing of projects coming to the market.
● Constraints on development opportunities.
● Public sector initiatives/investment.

The timing of projects coming to the market

104   The property market is highly cyclical and it is, therefore, difficult to disentangle the impact of a grant aided development from the normal action of the market.

105   The Hartlepool Business Park for example was completed in the third quarter of 1990 when the market was in recession. The relative failure of this project either to attract occupiers or to induce further development may relate more to the timing of the scheme coming to the market than the product being wrong.

106 By contrast the successful Snowhill Station in Birmingham was completed in a market where no new office development had occurred for a number of years and there was an existing office supply of over 500,000 sf. Although this scheme was very successful, surprisingly, no further new office development occurred in Birmingham until 18 months after it was completed and sold, by which time the property boom was in full flow.

107 3–5 St Pauls Square in Birmingham is perhaps the best example from our sample of induced investment. This development supplemented small scale private sector investment in the area and removed an environmental detractor. This had the effect of changing developers perceptions of the area, which had not previously been considered for office development. This improved the area sufficiently to be considered a viable office location when the development boom arrived.

Constraints on Development Opportunities

108 Induced investment can only occur where there are no constraints which preclude development. Typical constraints in an inner city location may include land ownership, the poor quality of the existing urban fabric, or the high cost of reclamation. Even when land is available grant aided development still requires to demonstrate that the benefits of redevelopment outweigh the existing use value of the site.

109 In the case of the Courtaulds warehouse in Hull, the tight urban fabric of the Old Town limited the extent to which it was possible to induce new development. It did, however, assist in encouraging private owners to improve the maintenance and repair of their buildings and has, therefore, induced a degree of additional investment into the area.

110 The Rutland Square Hotel development in Nottingham is similar, where land available for additional development is limited. There has, however, again been an improvement in the fabric of neighbouring properties and the Local Authority has observed an increase in the take up of refurbishment grants.

111 Even where a grant-aided scheme enhances the likelihood of development in an area, this may still be insufficient to overcome underlying constraints such as contamination. Southglade Park, Nottingham for example, achieved a high level of enhanced sales value on completion. However, the adjoining site still remains undeveloped as a result of high reclamation cost. Although market conditions have dictated that actual development has not been induced as a result of this scheme the likelihood of the adjoining site being developed in the near future has been substantially improved.

112 Similarly in Felling Town Centre, Gateshead, the development of a new shopping and commercial facility has improved the opportunities for development of a vacant site fronting the pedestrian High Street. At the time of writing this report Gateshead Metropolitan Borough Council (GMBC), the owners of the site, are preparing to place the site on the market for development. The fact that this step can be contemplated in today's extremely depressed conditions speaks volumes.

Public Sector Initiatives/Investment

113 Public sector initiatives/investment in an area represent additional public sector resources being spent often to achieve similar objectives to City Grant. As these schemes have similar aims and objectives and are often undertaken over the same time frame it is difficult to determine whether subsequent investment decisions have been influenced by a specific City Grant scheme or by a range of improvements in the area.

114 We have listed below a number of examples from our sample where City Grant schemes and other public sector initiatives worked in tandem to improve the local area and to attract further private sector investment.

115 In Felling Town Centre, (GMBC) prepared a policy statement in 1982 envisaging a phased revitalisation of the High Street and assisted the eventual City Grant aided development by use of compulsory purchase powers to acquire the site. The council also designated a Shopping Improvement Area where grants were made available for physical upgrading of the remaining retail units.

116 In Leicester the City Council promoted the New Walk Area as an attractive office location by awarding grants for physical improvements to historic buildings. A few minutes walk away from this is a cluster of 3 grant aided schemes (St Johns Corner) including Arnhem House.

117 In Newcastle, the Newcastle Initiative built on Newcastle City Council's earlier initiative to retain Grey Street as the commercial heart of the City. The City Grant for 43–49 Grey Street, although influential, was not the first scheme in the street to tackle an important building with grant assistance.

118 In all of these examples City Grant was considered to have had a positive impact on the wider regeneration of the area and to have made a valuable contribution to other public sector initiatives in the area.

Conclusion

119   It is clear from our interviews with developers, local authorities and property agents that the majority of schemes had a positive demonstration effect and helped to change other investors' perceptions of the inner area. It is, however, not possible to be quantitative about the level of additional investment these schemes induced. The rapid escalation in property values in the mid to late 1980's along with other public sector initiatives make determination of the impact of an individual scheme impossible to isolate.

IMPACT ON LAND VALUES

120   The impact of grant aid on land values is a difficult and contentious issue which has provoked considerable debate between public and private sectors. Existing land values are also perceived to be a significant constraint to inner city development and regeneration.

121   The DoE view is quite clear and has been explicitly stated in successive City Grant Guidance Notes. The following extracts have been taken from the 1992 Guidance Notes

122   "City Grant will not be offered on projects when the costs include unreasonably high site values or where the site value forms an unacceptably large proportion of the total grant requirement".

123   It goes on to say that

> "if the site value is high it may be reasonable to assume that the land or buildings can be used or developed without grant" and in "considering site values the appraiser will ask what the site is likely to fetch if sold now, in its existing physical condition, for use or for any likely permitted development, and on the assumption that grant will not be available".

124   While this approach is aimed at preventing the benefit of grant aid being fed directly through to the land owner, it does not always encourage inner city land to be brought forward for redevelopment and therefore facilitate regeneration.

125   We have assessed the impact of grant aid on land values as follows;

- Has grant aid resulted in increased land values on surrounding sites.
- Do unrealistic land values prevent City Grant bringing forward regeneration.

Has Grant Aid Increased Land Values?

126   In determining whether grant aid has increased land values it is important to distinguish which land values we are considering and whether increased land value are desirable or not. We have assessed this as follows:

(i)   land values in grant appraisal
(ii) the effect of grant aid on surrounding land values

127   D.O.E. guidance on land values for appraisal purposes is quite clear, in that values must not exceed existing use value, ignoring the impact of grant availability. This is consistent with the aim of providing support to overcome unique inner city problems and not simply to unlock development sites at any cost.

128   The effect of grant aid on surrounding land values is difficult to isolate and may or may not be desirable. If land values and capital values rise as a result of the demonstration effect of a grant aided project to the extent that unaided development can be undertaken then grant is achieving the dual aims of bring forward development activity and encouraging landowners to dispose of surplus inner city sites. If, however, it simply results in the landowners perceptions that his site value has increased (hope value) then this will act as a deterrent to development.

129   In an attempt to assess this we asked the developer of each City Grant project, local authorities and estate agents whether specific City Grant aided schemes had directly led to an increase in land values in the immediate neighbourhood. In every case they said that it had not, although this required to be considered in the context of the property market conditions pertaining at the time.

130   In practice, however our research indicated that over time values in areas immediately adjacent to some City Grant schemes have shown growth, although this is normally where a number of schemes have been undertaken or a combination of initiatives have produced a demonstration effect and increased developers confidence. Examples of this are the Lace Market in Nottingham and St Johns Corner in Leicester. This should not be considered a "bad thing" as it shows that grant aided schemes are contributing to creating a viable development market which had not previously existed.

131   Our conclusion is that specific grant aided schemes have not directly fuelled increases in land values, although they have assisted when combined with other initiatives in increasing confidence in an area, which has in the long term led to growth in land values. Whether this has been sufficient to encourage

land owners to dispose of surplus sites or whether it has prevented regeneration is discussed in the next section.

Do Unrealistic Land Values Prevent Grant Aid Bringing Forward Regeneration?

132 Having established that 'specific' grant aided projects have not directly lead to increased land values we now turn to whether unrealistic land values prevent regeneration.

133 In order to assess the effect of land values on grant applications we have analysed in the table 2.1 below land values as a percentage of the grant approved and also as a percentage of the total cost of the scheme.

134 Excluding the Archbishop Temple Business Units in Southwark, the analysis of land value as a percentage of total grant shows a range from 0% of total grant awarded to 92%. This raises the question of what is meant in the guidance notes in relation to land values as "an unacceptably large proportion of the total grant requirement". The analysis of land as a proportion of total development cost, again excluding Archbishop Temple Business Units, produces a narrower range of between 0% and 17% with the majority being under 10%.

Table 2.1 – Land value analysis					
Project Name	Grant Approved	Land Value as appraised	Land Value as a % of Grant Approved	Total Cost	Land Value as a % of Total Cost
Leicester, Arnhem House	£708,000	£200,000	28%	£6,787,275	3%
Manchester, Albion House	£301,000	£75,000	25%	£1,479,400	5%
Newcastle, 43/49 Grey St	£487,500	£406,435	83%	£4,147,500	10%
Sheffield, Huttons Buildings	£269,750	£0	0%	£1,789,891	0%
Southwark, Archbishop Temple Business Units	£500,000	£1,000,000	200%	£4,098,560	24%
Birmingham, Garrison Lane	£570,000	£261,000	46%	£3,476,000	8%
Birmingham, Startpoint	£283,000	£195,000	69%	£1,133,000	17%
Hartlepool Bus Park	£634,600	£110,000	17%	£4,574,000	2%
Southwark, Priter Way Arches	£525,000	£80,000	15%	£3,025,000	3%
Birmingham One Stop Perry Bar	£2,620,000	£2,400,000	92%	£21,684,164	11%
Bolton, Bark Street	£4,500,000	£0	0%	£37,540,000	0%
Gateshead, Felling Town Centre	£575,000	£255,000	44%	£2,777,000	9%
Middlesbrough, Zetland Road	£661,000	£5,000	1%	£3,100,760	0%
Manchester, Midland Hotel	£2,200,000	£0	0%	£13,037,000	0%
Nottingham, Rutland Square Hotel	£738,000	£235,000	32%	£3,216,000	7%
TOTAL	£15,572,250	£5,222,435	33%	£111,868,000	5%

135 On average land value as a percentage of grant awarded is 33% which is slightly higher than the DoE's own analysis of all 281 City Grant cases which have been approved and not subsequently cancelled or withdrawn, at 27%. A reason for this could be that our sample included an unusually high proportion of sites with visible buildings and existing use values would relate to both the site and buildings.

136 The question is do applicants' unrealistically high aspirations for land value prevent grant awards being made? The answer to this is undoubtably yes because appraisers insist on using existing use values and do not allow inflated land values resulting from the availability of City Grant. The wide variations in appraised site value as a percentage of grant reflects at one extreme appraisers success in imposing zero/nominal site values where there is no existing/potential use without grant, and at the other extreme City Grant's ability to take on and upgrade sites with existing but undervalued buildings.

137 Difficulties arise when landowners will not accept existing use values as they perceive their site to have a higher value. This is known as 'hope value' and can prevent inner city sites being brought forward for development. Hope value can be rationalised as a landowner's perception of the value of his land or building at sometime in the future discounted back to today's date. If an offer for the site meets his perception of value he will sell, if not, he will hold onto the site.

138 Unfortunately although the theory can be rationalised, individuals' perceptions of future worth are rarely below the existing use value. This is exacerbated by the fact that the "do nothing option" although having an opportunity cost to the landowner, in many cases will not have serious financial implications in absolute terms. Selling land is unlikely to be the principal business of an inner city landowner and sites and building will often have been on a company's books for a considerable number of years and may be included at very low values. From the landowner's perspective, there is no urgency to dispose of the site especially if there are prospects (no matter how remote) of receiving substantially more for the site (new planning permission, etc) at some future date.

139 In one sense this may not be an issue for City Grant, as it is a demand led grant i.e. if this scheme does not proceed then the private sector will bring forward another scheme which will take up the resources. This is true as long as the take up for City Grant remains high (which it has to date) and the projects which are prevented from occurring do not act as a major constraint to further inner city regeneration.

140 If the private sector is perceived to be constraining regeneration, then the issue may be how best to persuade them to dispose of their land at what is considered a fair value. This raises a number of contentious issues regarding public sector intervention in the working of the property market. The principal means of public sector intervention are directly through the use of compulsory purchase powers or indirectly through either planning powers or taxation.

141 The answer as far as City Grant has been concerned, has been to reject schemes where site values cannot be justified by reference to existing use values. While accepting the level of existing use values can be influenced by the nature and extent of buildings on a site our analysis (Table 2.1) suggest that a degree of flexibility is being allowed in the interpretation of this approach.

142 While we are aware that there are set procedures which appraisers use when assessing land values in City Grant applications, we also recognise that rigid adherence to this can prevent regeneration occurring.

CONCLUSION

143 City Grant projects (in combination with other initiatives) have clearly had an impact on the value of surrounding land and buildings either by raising values over time or by raising owners perception of value. What is not clear is whether City Grant has encouraged the release of inner city sites or inadvertently prevented sites from being developed. Strict adherence at appraisal to existing use values is unlikely to encourage owners, who perceive that the value of their land has increased, to dispose of their sites for less than they consider they are worth, especially where the costs of holding are not significant in absolute terms.

144 Successful City Grant projects may therefore be fuelling surrounding landowners perception of the value of their sites but as these values will not be eligible in a City Grant application this may result in land not being disposed of and therefore regeneration being prevented.

3 ECONOMIC IMPACT

INTRODUCTION

145 The purpose of this chapter is to assess the net economic impact of the non housing projects sampled in both phases of our research.

146 For those Government programmes targeted directly on employment creation, cost per job must be the primary measure of cost effectiveness. Employment creation is one of the principal objectives of City Grant and therefore we have made a detailed study of the cost per net additional job. We have based this on an extensive survey programme which has targeted each occupier in all of the sampled projects (see Appendix 1). Where appropriate we have supplemented this using the responses to the developer questionnaires and by knowledge gained during field visits and discussions with planning authority officials and local property agents.

THEORETICAL FRAMEWORK

147 Before describing the methodology we have used to analyse responses to questionnaires we set out below a full theoretical approach to calculate the employment generation effects of Central Government expenditure at the sub national level. The approach is summarised in Figure 3.1. It must, however, be remembered that even in the case of commercial and industrial projects, City Grant has wider objectives than just creating jobs. It is also concerned with land reclamation and with environmental benefits, therefore cost per job, whilst the primary measure of effectiveness does not reflect all of the benefits generated by City Grant expenditure.

The full approach

148 The first stage in this theoretical approach calculates the *Gross Employment Effects* from the initial policy expenditure. Gross employment has three distinct sources.

The first comprises all *direct employment* in the economic activity housed in the assisted project. The second source is *indirect employment* which is derived from backward and forward supply linkages established with local supplying and purchasing companies.

The final source is from *Construction Employment* generated during the creation of the physical project.

149 The last of these categories is considered as temporary employment whilst, unless evidence to the contrary is provided, the first two categories are assumed to be sources of permanent employment.

150 To arrive at a figure for *Net Employment Creation* two potential detractors need to be quantified and subtracted from the gross employment figure.

151 The first of these is *Deadweight*, which exists where similar (or in some cases equivalent) project outputs would have been secured for the sub national area in the absence of public sector assistance. In the case of City Grant if a particular development would have proceeded without grant then all outputs generated represent Deadweight and the net employment effects are zero.

152 The second potential detractor is *Displacement* which occurs where;

- gross jobs in the project previously existed in the local area
- where alternative non assisted projects in the relevant area could have sustained the employment generated by new investors (and remained capable of doing so at the time of survey)

153 To arrive at an estimate of *Net Employment Creation* the appropriate levels of Deadweight and Displacement are subtracted from the figure for Gross Employment Creation.

154 In addition there are the multiplier effects which need to be considered following calculation of Net Employment Creation to arrive at the net additional effect on the economy of the relevant area.

155 In the short term there will be an *Income Multiplier* which will reflect the additional economic activity generated from the expenditure of new employees living and working in the relevant area.

156 In the longer term linkages will be established from assisted companies to incoming and existing companies, bringing additional economic gains and

employment to the relevant area. This is known as the *Economic Development Multiplier*.

157   The *Net Additionality* of the public sector assistance is therefore expressed as the total Full Time Equivalent jobs from Net Employment Creation plus the multiplier effects identified over the short and long terms.

158   This figure is then used as the denominator to arrive at the prime measure of value for money – the *Net Cost Per Job*.

The DoE approach

159   For the purposes of assessing the economic impact of City Grant we have adopted the Department of Environment's simplified version of the full model (see Figure 2). This is based on the DoE guidance notes issued in June 1991 for measuring ex ante appraisal and ex post evaluation of sub national projects and policies. The Guidance Notes referred to were issued by F.A.C.T. Department of Environment in June 1991. Although this guidance refers to both ex ante appraisal and ex post evaluation it is not used for City Grant appraisals. This is because of the difficulty in assessing displacement ex ante. Until the occupier is identified it is impossible to accurately predict the level of net additional jobs. This has led to the development by the City Grant appraisers of an "aim off technique" (see paragraph 190) at appraisal. For the purpose of our ex post appraisal, and with the benefit of having identified the occupiers, the FACT methodology is appropriate.

160   For the purposes of this report, and in line with the DoE approach we have not considered;

Temporary Jobs

161   Construction jobs and other temporary jobs have not been considered in our review. Paragraph 16 of the DoE guidance notes advises that temporary and construction jobs should not be included in the calculation of economic input and value for money. The guidance notes advise that it is usually impossible to forecast the number of construction jobs at the appraisal stage and, moreover, that difficulties in forecasting the duration of permanent jobs mean it is not possible to standardise temporary jobs to permanent equivalents and add them to permanent employment creation.

162   Temporary jobs are therefore excluded from our analysis of economic impact in this chapter and in assessing value for money in Chapter 6.

Multiplier Effects and indirect jobs

163   Short term income multiplier effects, the longer term economic development multipliers and indirect jobs have not been considered in this review of City Grant. **DoE guidance notes (paragraph 25) specifically state that such effects should be excluded as estimation is speculative, and experience suggests that the measured multiplier does not vary greatly between projects and therefore will not affect the ranking of projects for selection purposes**.

METHODOLOGY

164   The application of the DoE theoretical framework to the task of establishing the economic impact of the sample projects is described in the following paragraphs.

Figure 3.2 Summarises this approach which in essence omits temporary jobs, indirect jobs and the multiplier effects. Figure 3.1 provides a comparison with a wider approach to calculating and total outputs and value for money.

165   For each individual respondent the starting point was the number of permanent gross jobs in their premises at the time of the survey. Respondents provided information on full time and part time permanent jobs and these have been adjusted to Full Time Equivalent (FTE) jobs. Part time jobs were categorised as those providing less than 24 hours employment per week. We have assumed that respondents would not register any employees working less than 7.5 hours per week. Adopting the mid point between these ranges (15.75 hours) and approximating this to the average full working week (37.5 hours) we estimate a part time job to equate to 42% of a full time job. We have applied this reduction factor to permanent part time jobs and added these to full time positions to arrive at an estimate of FTE jobs.

166   For multi-occupant projects, responses were aggregated and supplemented to include estimates of gross jobs for non-respondents. Estimates apply the ratio of employees housed per square foot in respondent's premises to other occupied, but non-responding, units within the same development. Necessary adjustments are made to ensure that the ratios applied produce a reasonable approximation, given the use and size of premises occupied by non-respondents.

167   We have chosen in both phases of the study to ignore any potential employment benefits to be gained from the future occupation of currently vacant units. We believe this to be a reasonable and valid assumption given that at the time of the survey

Figure 3.1   The full approach to estimating the outturn employment effects of central government employment generation expenditure

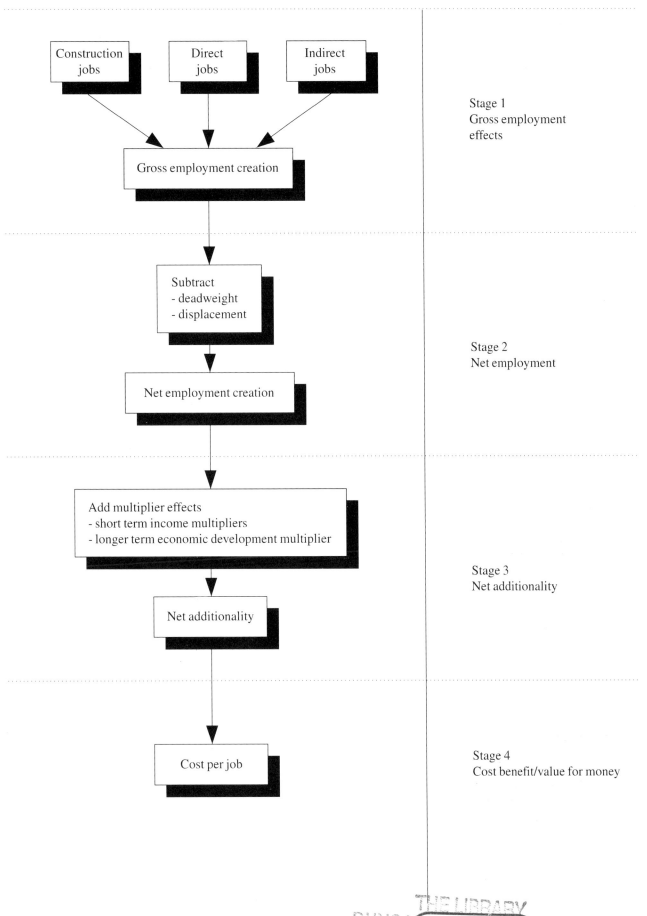

Figure 3.2   The DOE's recommended simplified method

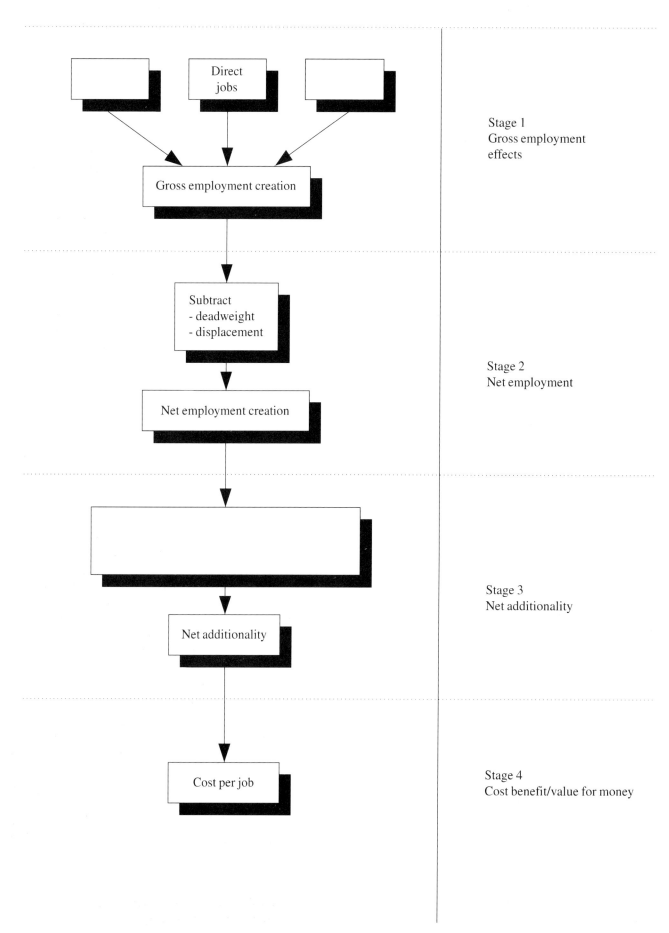

Direct
jobs

Gross employment creation

Stage 1
Gross employment
effects

Subtract
- deadweight
- displacement

Net employment creation

Stage 2
Net employment

Net additionality

Stage 3
Net additionality

Cost per job

Stage 4
Cost benefit/value for money

all of the projects had been completed and exposed to the market for a minimum of six months.

168 The information available from the sample has enabled us to include allowances for deadweight and displacement in our ex post analysis. These have been calculated as follows:

Deadweight

169 The first test applied is the need for grant, measured from responses to developer questionnaires, where respondents were asked to comment on the likelihood of their developments proceeding in the absence of an award of grant. Jobs in projects which are identified as not having required Grant would need to be categorised as Deadweight.

Displacement

170 In theory displacement arises where a company makes a decision to locate in assisted premises rather than other available premises within the inner area. The employment effects of any firm which moves into grant aided premises *from other premises in the inner area* are considered as displacement; the exceptions being:

- growth in employment since occupation;
- new jobs created on occupation;
- retained jobs (jobs which would have been lost if the firm had not moved).

171 The employment effects of *new firms* or *firms originally located outside the inner area* which move into grant aided premises are treated as displacement if the firm considered that other suitable premises already existed in the area. We assume that in such cases the firm would have moved into the area anyway in the absence of grant aided premises. Inward moving firms which did not think that alternative suitable premises existed are assumed to be net additions because they would not have moved to the inner area if the grant aided premises had not existed.

Figure 3.3 below illustrates the process used to calculate Displacement.

Figure 3.3   Displacement or net additional employment?

	Did you consider alternative premises in the inner area?	
	YES	**NO**
Firms from inner area	displacement	displacement
Inward investors	displacement	net additional employment

172 In the first phase analysis all gross jobs by respondents who had considered that there were alternative suitable premises in the Inner Area were categorised as displacement. In the second phase analysis this approach was refined and only those premises less than 10 years old were considered as real alternatives to the assisted premises. It is accepted that even with this refinement this is a relatively crude measure of displacement. However attempts to improve on its accuracy would involve second guessing location decisions made by occupiers at a point in time (often several years previously) within a dynamic property market. This approach would greatly extend research effort and could not be guaranteed to provide a more accurate result.

173 This approach tends to generate lower figures for net additional jobs and a higher cost per job than would emerge from the "aim off technique" (see paragraph 190) because it uses hindsight to make more accurate deductions for deadweight and displacement. It is of course arguable that in a full ex post assessment we should balance this by adding more explicit allowances for construction and multiplier effects, but this was outside our brief.

The Sample

174 As explained in Chapter 1 the sample was chosen to cover a range of completed projects to draw out best practice lessons, not as a statistically representative sample of the programme as a whole.

175 We have chosen to analyse the combined results of the Phase 1 and Phase 2 Surveys on a sectoral basis with reporting of findings for Industrial, Office, Retail, and Hotel schemes. This will allow for cross-sectoral comparison of assistance in both this chapter and the value for money chapter of our report. Table 3.4 below shows the proportion of each category of scheme in the sample.

Table 3.4 – Sample analysis		
Use Type	No	%
Industrial	11	37
Hotel	3	10
Office	10	33
Retail	6	20
Total	30	100

176 We will consider each of these categories in turn under the following headings

Gross Employment Creation

Net Employment Creation

- Deadweight
- Displacement
- Other Effects

Conclusions

GROSS EMPLOYMENT CREATION

177 It is estimated that 5,271 FTE gross jobs (4,677 full time and 1,386 part time) were housed in sample schemes at the respective survey dates for Phases 1 and 2. Table 3.5 shows the gross employment breakdown by sector.

Table 3.5 – Gross jobs housed by sector		
Use Type	Gross jobs	%
Office	1,490	28%
Industrial	1,889	36%
Retail	1,203	23%
Hotel	689	13%
All	5,271	100%

178 Tables 3.6 – 3.9 set out employment and floorspace details for each scheme in each of the use type sectors analysed.

Table 3.6 – Industrial schemes				
Scheme	Area Occupied SF	Gross jobs	% of Total	SF Per Employee
Birmingham, Garrison Lane	40,226	80	4.2	503
Birmingham, IMI Holford	522,648	894	47.3	585
Birmingham, Newhall Hill	15,000	95	5.0	158
Birmingham, Startpoint Industrial Units	40,889	90	4.8	454
Boldon Business Park	100,777	199	10.5	506
Hartlepool, Hartlepool Business Park	15,470	29	1.5	533
Nottingham, Beechdale Engineering	77,000	220	11.7	350
Nottingham, Southglade Park	50,400	92	4.9	548
Oldham, MCM Ltd	6,394	25	1.3	256
Oldham, Stamford Mill	29,800	161	8.5	185
Southwark, Priter Way Arches	7,115	4	0	1779
TOTAL	905,719	1,889	100.0	480

Table 3.7 – Office schemes				
Scheme	Area Occupied SF	Gross jobs	% of Total	SFT Per Employee
Birmingham, 3–5 St Pauls Sq	19,500	10	0.7	195
Birmingham, Snowhill Station	41,000	472	31.7	87
Leicester, Arnhem House	55,000	279	18.8	197
Manchester, Albion House	18,350	9	0.6	2039
Newcastle, 43/49 Grey St	10,827	27	1.8	401
Nottingham, Newcastle House	67,000	250	16.8	268
Nottingham, Stoney Street	25,000	200	13.4	125
Oldham, Union Street	25,712	46	3.1	559
Sheffield, Huttons Buildings	18,804	75	5.0	251
Southwark, Archbishop Temple Units	24,514	122	8.1	201
TOTAL	305,707	1,490	100.0	205

Table 3.8 – Retail schemes				
Scheme	Area Occupied SF	Gross jobs	% of Total	SFT Per Employee
Birmingham, One Stop Perry Bar	291,676	516	42.9	565
Bolton, Bark Street	231,556	389	32.3	595
Gateshead, Felling Town Centre	38,505	81	6.7	475
Hull, Bransholme North	14,240	66	5.5	216
Middlesbrough, Zetland Road	20,956	125	10.4	168
South Shields, Catherine Street	15,151	26	2.2	606
TOTAL	612,084	1,203	100.0	509

Table 3.9 – Hotel schemes				
Scheme	Bedrooms	Employees Housed	% of Total	Employees Per Room
Birmingham, Paradise Circus	181	257	37.3	1.42
Manchester, Midland Hotel	303	343	49.8	1.13
Nottingham, Rutland Square Hotel	103	89	12.9	0.86
TOTAL	587	689	100.0	1.17

179 The ratios of area to employees housed are set out in Table 3.10 below. These figures might be usefully applied in future ex-ante appraisal techniques as a basis for verifying the estimates of gross jobs used in support of applications for grant.

Table 3.10	
Scheme Type	SFT Per Employee
Office	205
Industrial	479
Retail	509
Hotel	–
ALL	387

180 An analysis of the proportions of part time and full time gross jobs serves to highlight the differences between the types of use undertaken in assisted schemes. Table 3.11 provides an analysis of part time and full time gross jobs in each scheme type.

Table 3.11		
Scheme Type	Full Time (%)	Part Time (%)
Office	92.9	7.1
Industrial	92.4	7.6
Retail	45.3	54.7
Hotel	78.2	21.8
ALL	77.1	22.9

181 We do not consider in this section the relative value for money and effectiveness of individual schemes or types of scheme as these issues are considered in detail in Chapter 6 "Value for Money".

NET EMPLOYMENT CREATION

182 From the responses to questionnaires and our estimate of gross jobs, we generate, in the following sections, our estimate of net employment created by the sample schemes which is additional to the appropriate inner area. To arrive at this figure we estimate deadweight and displacement for each of the sample schemes and deduct the appropriate allowance from the total numbers of gross jobs.

Estimating deadweight in the sample

183 As previously stated Deadweight comprises all employment housed in those schemes which would

have occurred either in the timescale proposed in the original grant application, or fairly shortly afterwards even if grant had not been made available. In our interviews with the developers of schemes in both samples we did not identify any scheme which would have been completed in the proposed timescale in the absence of an award of grant. We therefore conclude that Deadweight does not exist for any of the schemes in our sample. The tables for each scheme included in this chapter do not therefore make reference to Deadweight.

Estimating displacement in the sample

184 As stated in our methodology the calculation of Displacement requires us to distinguish between both inward and indigenous occupiers, and whether occupants considered alternative premises. Firstly, by asking for the old address of an occupier we were able to identify all firms which had moved from within the inner area. These were then classed as displacement. Secondly, for all inward investors to the inner area, we asked whether they considered suitable alternative premises in the inner area (for Phase II we refined our questionnaire to ask whether these premises were less than 10 yrs old). If they did, they were also classed as displacement. Those which did not were assumed to be net additional. We also took account of growth in employment since occupation, new jobs created on occupation and retained jobs.

Net Effect (Net Employment Generation)

185 Net employment generation can now be calculated by deducting deadweight and displacement from the estimates of gross employment in the sample schemes. This gives net employment figures as shown in table 3.12.

186 It should be stressed that these figures represent *post hoc estimates* of net employment generated in the inner area. This estimate has been based on the responses from the questionnaires which have been grossed up to represent the whole sample (respondents represented projects accounting for 76% of total gross employment).

187 For the sample as a whole we estimate that of all gross jobs, some 46% can be classified as Displacement. The percentages in the last column of Table 3.12 show the proportion of net additional jobs to the inner area from the total gross jobs in assisted schemes. The seemingly high levels of additionality for retail and hotel schemes are influenced to some extent by the importance of location for each of these activities and by the relative scarcity of alternative premises within the inner area. Whilst

Table 3.12 – Aggregated Results for Sample				
Scheme Type	Gross Employment	Less Displacement	Net Employment	Net Employment as Proportion of Gross (%)
Office	1,490	1,068	422	28.3%
Industrial	1,889	877	1,012	53.6%
Retail	1,203	394	809	67.2%
Hotel	689	77	612	88.8%
ALL	5,271	2,416	2,855	54.2%

there may be many potential locations for office or industrial premises in an inner area the number of commercially viable sites for retail or hotel use will be more restricted, due to their greater reliance on passing trade and the existence of historically more restrictive planning policies. Occupants of office and industrial schemes appear to have a greater propensity to consider alternatives. This may however be a function of the availability of a greater number of alternative choices for these uses.

188 Whilst these figures might be usefully applied as a proxy for potential employment in schemes presented for appraisal, we would caution against applying them rigidly to specific schemes. The figures could not be used as an acid test but may be useful in determining whether estimates produced in support of appraisals are realistic or optimistic.

189 In addition to considering employment creation as a measure of economic impact (as highlighted in the DoE guidelines) we have also considered other indicators of economic impacts which could be used to present a more comprehensive view of the economic effects of the policy. These are shown in appendix 2 and include the analysis of the source of business, location of competitors, customers and suppliers, and local population impacts for the occupiers of the grant aided schemes.

COMPARISON OF ESTIMATED OUTTURN JOBS WITH THOSE PROJECTED AT THE TIME OF THE GRANT APPROVAL

Projected and actual jobs created

190 We estimated the gross jobs housed and net additional jobs created in the grant aided projects using the DOE recommended method for ex post analysis of job creating programmes. We then compared this with the number of jobs forecast by the appraisers at the time of the grant application. As they were working ex ante they took a still more simplified approach. They estimated gross jobs that could be accommodated in the completed premises –

by reference to the floor area and the expected type of use. They then deducted:

(i) jobs already on the site, if any;
(ii) jobs which could be expected to arise from the next best use of the site – if the site value used in the appraisal implied that there *were* alternative uses;
(iii) known transfers – in cases where the project was to be pre-let to a firm moving from elsewhere in the inner area.

191 This method does not attempt to estimate wider displacement effects which of course could not be known before the project was built or the occupier identified. But to compensate for this, the Department adopted unusually low cost per job guidelines. The average *appraised* cost per job on approved applications was only £5,000 and few projects were approved where the forecast cost per job at the appraisal stage was greater than £10,000. The intention was to set low cost per job limits to compensate for the likelihood that ex post appraisal would show larger displacement losses. The City Grant appraisers refer to this as the "Aim Off Technique" and it affects the interpretation of the costs per job in Chapter 6 below.

192 Because grants were only offered when the appraisal indicated that, without grant, the project would not proceed at all, it was not necessary for the appraisers to make any deduction for deadweight.

193 Despite these fundamental differences between the appraisers' ex ante forecasts and our ex post analysis, it is useful to compare the results. Table 3.13 shows, that taking the sample as a whole, the net additional jobs on the basis of our ex post appraisal amounted to only 45% of those forecast ex ante by the appraisers. Setting aside hotels, where the appraisers *underestimated*, the other projects achieved only 38% of the ex ante forecast of net additional jobs.

194 It is clear that in these sampled cases and even after allowing for the "Aim Off" the Department did not

Table 3.13 – Projected and actual job creation by use type					
	Projected jobs at appraisal	Actual Gross Jobs	Gross as % of Projected	Actual Net Jobs	Net as % of Projected
Offices	1,320	1,490	113%	422	32%
Industrial	2,538	1,889	74%	1,012	40%
Retail	2,003	1,203	60%	809	44%
Hotels	410	689	168%	612	150%
Total	6,271	5,271	84%	2,855	45%

make sufficient allowance for displacement losses. We are aware that procedures have been tightened up over the last two or three years but think there is room for further improvement. The Department will wish to continue to keep the system simple but we suggest that, if the existing technique is retained, the appraisers, in producing their ex ante forecasts, should include a deduction for displacement. This could be estimated after analysing previous case papers on a sectoral and regional basis. This would give a better estimate of the likely extent of displacement. The consequence of this of course is that if a similar mix of projects is to be approved, (and given the range of other benefits produced there seems to be no reason to seek to alter that mix), a rather higher ex ante cost per job will have to be accepted.

CONCLUSIONS

195 From our review of the economic impact of City Grant we have drawn the following conclusions. These are of a general nature and relate to the sample analysed. We would wish to emphasise that our analysis has considered the sample as a whole and our findings should not be applied rigidly to the appraisal of individual schemes. The conclusions are potentially of use as a guide to any future redesign of City Grant or other proposed property development assistance scheme.

196 The schemes in the sample housed a total of 5,271 Full Time Equivalent jobs at the respective survey dates. Of these 2,851 FTE jobs (54.1%) were calculated as being net additional to the inner area.

197 Office schemes in the sample housed an estimated total of 1,490 jobs of which 422 (28.3%) were additional. This was the lowest level of additionality achieved in any category. Industrial schemes in the sample housed an estimated total of 1,889 jobs of which 1,012 (53.6%) were additional. This level of additionality approximates closely to the average for the whole sample. Retail schemes in the sample housed an estimated total of 1,203 jobs of which 809 (67.2%) were additional. This was the second highest level of additionality for the sample. Hotel schemes in the sample housed an estimated total of 689 employees with a very high number – 612 (88.8%) identified as additional to the inner area.

198 We have noted the contrast between the numbers of jobs forecast at the time of the appraisal and the much lower number which, with our advantage of hindsight, we judge to be net additional jobs. We think the Department should make more allowance for displacement in its appraisals.

4 Environmental Impact

INTRODUCTION

199 The majority of the grant appraisals for the projects in our sample identified environmental benefits as an important objective or an anticipated benefit of the project.

200 We have adopted an approach which quantifies scores against measurable indicators and attempts to gauge a number of more qualitative assessments of environmental impact. Our approach builds on the earlier work of Aston University (1988) and Pieda which developed approaches to evaluate the environmental impact of UDG and LEG-UP funded projects respectively.

201 We have divided our analysis into two levels of environmental impact:

- On Site changes
- Off Site changes in the surrounding area

SITE LEVEL CHANGES

Introduction

202 At the grant appraisal stage 28 out of 36 projects were set objectives that were either expressly, or by implication, related to the achievement of environmental benefits. Within this group ten mentioned environmental objectives directly whilst the remainder included statements such as "to restore a Listed Building", "develop a derelict site" or "enhance a Conservation area" all of which bestow environmental benefits.

203 The environmental impact of site level changes is dependent on a wide range of factors which together indicate the extent to which a site has been improved. The site level impact has been assessed on the basis of the extent to which people (residents, motorists and passers by) benefit from the improvement. Factors which we have attempted to assess are:

- Size of project
- Visibility and prominence
- Removal of dereliction

- Reduction of detractors
- Environmental/building conservation
- Increased usage of site
- Quality of design
- Traffic and parking
- Pollution

204 Where appropriate each factor was scored on a scale of 0–5 with 0 representing, little or no impact and 5 a high level of improvement. Negative scores were also possible in some cases where there was an actual worsening in conditions.

Size of project

205 Two aspects of the size of projects were examined:

- The land area developed
- The number of square feet developed or refurbished.

Whilst different land uses tend to develop a site to a different intensity, larger sites tend nevertheless to accommodate larger amounts of floorspace. Table 4.1 below clearly illustrates this point. The most significant exceptions are both hotels Manchester (Midland Hotel) and Birmingham (Paradise Circus) which are on relatively small sites within the city centre.

Visual Impact

206 The scale of a project's visual impact relates primarily to two factors:

- Visibility
- Prominence

Visibility in this context relates to the number of people who see the scheme (frequency) and how long they are likely to see it for (intensity). There are assumed to be three main components which might contribute to the degrees of visibility of a scheme. These are:

- Passing vehicles (road and rail)
- Passing pedestrians
- Overlooking dwellings

Table 4.1 – Site area & size of scheme							
Summary		Floorspace (square feet)					
		Very Small	Small	Medium	Large	Very Large	All
Site Area (Hectares)		0–9,999	10,000 –49,000	50,000 –99,999	100,000 –249,999	–250,000	
Very Small	0–0.99	1	6	1	1	1	10
Small	1–1.99	2	4	5	0	1	12
Medium	2–4.99	0	2	4	1	1	8
Large	5–9.99	0	0	1	1	1	3
Very Large	10+	0	0	0	2	1	3
All		3	12	11	5	5	36

Prominence in this context is defined as the extent to which the building can be seen from a distance. This relates primarily to relative size, particularly height. Other factors, notably a difference in the colour or architectural style of the building, can also contribute to its prominence.

Visibility

207 The degree of visibility is dependent on a range of variables which include the proximity of the building to the potential viewer and the extent to which the view is obscured by other buildings, hoardings etc. However, for the purposes of simplification we have only assessed relative numbers of potential viewers for each of the three categories above.

208 One potential category of viewer excluded from our analysis is overlooking commercial or industrial buildings. The extent to which the occupants of buildings can and will look out of the window was considered too difficult to estimate. It was also considered that the occupants of buildings would contribute to both passing pedestrians and/or vehicles and thus "impact" upon these potential viewers for each would be to some extent taken into account.

209 The number of passing vehicles and pedestrians was estimated and findings were compiled in use type groupings. Offices, retail and hotels were, not surprisingly the most visible schemes as they tend to be either within the city centre or close to arterial roads.

210 Industrial and housing schemes tend to have a lower levels of passing visibility reflecting the tendency for such schemes to be located in the outer parts of the urban core and often away from main road frontages.

211 Table 4.2 summarises the results of our assessment overleaf. Most schemes examined (30 out of 36) were judged to have either medium or very high visibility. In the office, retail and hotel categories only Nottingham, Rutland Square was judged to have a low level of visibility.

212 The trend for industrial and housing schemes to be less visible than office, hotel and retail schemes is demonstrated in Table 4.3 below.

213 A surprisingly high level of non-housing schemes (66%) are overlooked by houses. Perhaps most surprisingly is that eight out of eleven industrial schemes are overlooked by houses. Table 4.4 below gives a breakdown of the level of overlooking dwellings across each of the use type sectors.

Prominence

214 Exactly half of the survey schemes (18 out of 36) were judged to be prominent, as they could either be seen from neighbouring streets or from various points throughout the neighbourhood.

Table 4.2 – Passing Visibility			
	Passing Pedestrians	Passing Vehicles	Overall passing visibility
OFFICES			
Birmingham, 3–5 St Paul's Square	4	4	4
Birmingham, Snowhill Station	5	5	5
Leicester, Arnhem House	4	4	4
Manchester, Albion House	3	4	4
Newcastle, 43/49 Grey Street	4	4	4
Nottingham, Newcastle House	3	5	4
Nottingham, Stoney Street	3	4	3
Oldham, Union Street	4	4	4
Sheffield, Huttons	4	4	4
Southwark, Archbishop Temple Business Units	3	4	3
INDUSTRIAL			
Birmingham, Garrison Lane	2	4	3
Birmingham, IMI Holdford Park	2	4	3
Birmingham, Newhall Hill	2	3	2
Birmingham, Startpoint Industrial Units	3	3	3
Boldon Business Park	0	2	1
Hartlepool, Hartlepool Business Park	1	3	2
Nottingham, Beechdale Engineering	1	2	1
Nottingham, Southglade Park	2	4	3
Oldham, MCM Ltd	2	4	3
Oldham, Stamford Mill	2	2	2
Southwark, Priter Way Arches	3	3	3
RETAIL			
Birmingham, One Stop, Perry Bar	3	4	4
Bolton, Bark Street	5	4	5
Gateshead, Felling Town Centre	4	3	4
Hull, Bransholme North	3	3	3
Middlesbrough, Zetland Road (also included office development)	4	5	5
South Shields, Catherine Street	4	4	4
HOTELS			
Birmingham, Paradise Circus (also included office development)	5	5	5
Manchester, Midland Hotel	4	5	5
Nottingham, Rutland Square Hotel	2	2	2

continued

Table 4.2 continued – Passing Visibility			
HOUSING			
Birmingham, The Parade	3	4	4
Hull, Coltman Street	3	3	3
Hull, Courtauld's Warehouse (also included retail development)	4	2	4
Nottingham, Mudella Court	3	2	3
Nottingham, Southglade Park	2	4	3
Oldham, Bank Top Mill	2	2	2

Congested = Very high = 5
Frequent = High = 4
Regular = Medium = 3
Occasional = Low = 2
Rare = Very low = 1
None = Non-existent = 0

Table 4.3 – Overall passing visibility							
Scheme Type	None	Very Low	Low	Medium	High	Very High	All
Offices	0	0	0	1	8	1	10
Industrial	0	2	3	6	0	0	11
Retail	0	0	1	0	3	2	6
Hotels	0	0	1	0	0	2	3
Housing	0	0	1	4	1	0	6
All	0	2	6	11	12	5	36

Table 4.4 – Visibility: Overlooking dwellings							
Scheme Type	None	Very Low	Low	Medium	High	Very High	Total
Offices	3	2	1	2	1	1	10
Industrial	3	0	0	3	2	3	11
Retail	3	0	0	1	0	2	6
Hotels	1	0	0	2	0	0	3
Housing	1	0	0	0	2	3	6
All	11	2	1	8	5	9	36

Over 30 = Very High 5
21–30 = High 4
11–20 = Medium 3
6–10 = Low 2
1–5 = Very Low 1
0 = None 0

Table 4.5 – Prominence							
			Prominence				
Scheme Type	None	Very Low	Low	Medium	High	Very High	Total
Offices	0	1	3	3	2	1	10
Industrial	0	5	3	2	0	1	11
Retail	0	0	1	3	2	0	6
Hotels	0	1	0	0	2	0	3
Housing	0	2	2	1	1	0	6
All	0	9	9	9	7	2	36

Key

Dominates skyline	=	Very High	= 5
Seen from several points outside neighbourhood	=	High	= 4
Seen from neighbourhood streets	=	Medium	= 3
Seen from ends of streets	=	Low	= 2
Seen from part of street	=	Very Low	= 1
Not visible from street	=	None	= 0

215 The remainder of the sample were judged to be not prominent as they could only be seen from either part of or the end of streets.

216 Nine schemes were found to be visible from outside the neighbourhood, one of which (Leicester, Arnhem House) was also deemed to dominate the skyline. Retail, office and hotel predominated in this group with only one housing scheme (Hull, Courtauld's Warehouse) and one industrial (Birmingham, IMI Holford Park) being deemed to have a high level of prominence.

217 Table 4.6 below demonstrates that schemes can be prominent even if they are not highly visible to passing pedestrians or vehicles.

Table 4.6 – Visibility and prominence							
			Overall Passing Visibility				
Prominence	None	Very Low	Low	Medium	High	Very High	All
	0	1	2	3	4	5	
Not visible from street	0	0	0	0	0	0	0
Seen from part of street	0	2	2	2	2	0	8
Seen from ends of street	0	0	2	5	2	1	10
Seen from neighbourhood streets	0	0	0	5	3	2	10
Seen from several points outside neighbourhood	0	0	2	0	3	2	7
Dominates skyline	0	0	0	0	1	0	1
All	0	2	6	12	11	1	36

Removal of derelict land of the projects involved

218 We define dereliction as land or buildings that are neglected, dilapidated or abandoned. At one level therefore all the sites can be placed in this category with the possible exception of Boldon Business Park and Beechdale Engineering, Nottingham. In the former case the project was developed on a former colliery site that had been reclaimed to a greenfield state. In the latter case a company in the inner area relocated to a reclaimed colliery site in order to safeguard jobs.

219 Over half of the sample (19 out of 36) involved development on sites that had been totally abandoned and from which no economic use was being derived.

220 Dereliction can however extend to sites which are only semi-utilised often occupied by short term marginal users. This results in land or buildings which detract from the urban environment.

221 Table 4.7 provides a breakdown of derelict land and buildings over the whole sample. For the purpose of

Table 4.7 – Development of sites with existing buildings		
	Action Taken	Comment
OFFICES		
Birmingham, 3–5 St Paul's Square	Refurbishment	Listed Buildings. Burnt out shell.
Manchester, Albion House	Refurbishment	Listed Buildings. Close to collapse.
Newcastle, 43/49 Grey Street	Refurbishment	Listed Building. Close to collapse
Nottingham, Newcastle House	Refurbishment	Listed Building. (part of site only).
Oldham, Union Street	Demolition	Former chapel in poor state of repair.
Sheffield, Huttons Buildings	Refurbishment	Former Cutlers warehouse.
Southwark, Archbishop Temple Business Units	Refurbishment	Former Victorian school building.
INDUSTRIAL		
Birmingham, Newhall Hill	Refurbishment	Listed Building
Birmingham, Startpoint Industrial Units	Refurbishment	Former pre-war industrial accommodation.
Southwark, Priter Way Arches	Refurbishment	Derelict railway arches
RETAIL		
Birmingham, One Stop, Perry Bar	Demolition	Under-used 1960s shopping centre and greyhound stadium.
Bolton, Bark Street	Refurbishment	Listed Building, Victorian Market Hall.
Gateshead, Felling Town Centre	Demolition	Former terrace of shops and open car park.
Middlesbrough, Zetland Road (also included office development)	Refurbishment (part)	Fire damaged redundant buildings.
South Shields, Catherine Street	Demolition	Semi-derelict shops in poor state of repair.
HOTELS		
Manchester, Midland Hotel	Refurbishment	Listed Building. Victorian 'landmark' hotel.
Nottingham, Rutland Square Hotel	Refurbishment	Old concrete and brick warehouse.
HOUSING		
Hull, Coltman Street	Refurbishment	Part of Victorian terrace.
Hull, Courtauld's Warehouse (also included retail development)	Refurbishment	Listed Building.
Nottingham, Mundella Court	Demolition	Victorian school in poor state of repair.

analysis this has been divided between purely derelict sites without buildings and ones where buildings were either demolished or retained and refurbished.

222 The table also describes the work undertaken on each property in greater detail and reveals that of the 15 schemes involving the refurbishment of buildings over half (8 out of 15) were Listed Buildings.

223 The remainder of the sample (15 out of 36) could be defined as projects which had been developed on empty sites (see Table 4.8 below) although six of them had an economic use as car parks.

Table 4.8 – Schemes with some form of dereliction (Prior to scheme)	
Severe dereliction	2
Major dereliction	2
Moderate dereliction	7
Minor dereliction	3
Superficial dereliction	1
	15

Reduction of detractors

224 In 30 out of 36 schemes the project reduced on-site detractors. The six cases where there is judged to be no reduction were either sites which involved the refurbishment of recently vacated buildings (Midland Hotel, Manchester, and Archbishop Temple Business Units, Southwark) or cleared "greenfield" sites (Beechdale Engineering,

Nottingham, Boldon Business Park and Hartlepool Business Park). Stoney Street, Nottingham was an extremely ugly bomb site style carpark within a Conservation Area.

225 In only four cases (Manchester, Albion House; Birmingham, Garrison Lane; Birmingham, One Stop Perry Bar; Gateshead, Felling Town Centre and Southwark, Priter Way Railway Arches) was there a significant reduction of detractors. Stoney Street was a major eyesore.

226 The bulk of the sample (26 out of 36) were classified as having resulted in the reduction of slight detractors although the classification is highly subjective and only relates to reference to photographic archives and the memories of developers and Local Authority Officers.

Increased usage of a site

227 All the sites were categorised as under-used prior to the scheme and have experienced an increase in usage following the completion of the scheme. Tables 4.9 documents the increased usage of sites for each type of scheme.

Quality of Design

228 Three elements of project quality were identified in terms of:

- Building design
- Hard Landscaping
- Soft Landscaping

Table 4.9 – Increased usage of site							
	No previous use to maximum economic	Significant under-use to maximum use	Significant under-use to almost full use	Significant increase in use	Slight increase in use	No change	All
Project type							
Offices	4	3	2	1	0	0	10
Industrial	10	0	1	0	0	0	11
Retail	2	1	3	0	0	0	6
Hotels	1	1	1	0	0	0	3
Housing	4	1	1	0	0	0	6
All	21	6	8	1	0	0	36

Building Design

229 The quality of the scheme was measured against the extent to which they met different design criteria. The elements considered are:

  – Strong visual impact
  – High quality materials and finishes
  – Improvement to the local "streetscene"

230 A scheme is considered to be excellent if it meets all of the criteria. Such a scheme would receive a score rating of 4. A scheme which failed to meet any of the criteria would receive a score of 0.

231 Most (25 out of 36) of the projects were found to have produced buildings of a good or excellent standard in that they met, three or four of the criteria.

232 Table 4.10 below summarises the findings over use-types and demonstrates that both industrial, office and hotel projects tend to produce schemes of slightly better quality. By contrast four of six housing schemes were on average of lower quality of lower quality and tender to satisfy few of the criteria to determine quality of design.

Hard landscaping

233 In 27 out of 36 cases the project included an element of hard landscaping. Quality in this element was measured in terms of:

  • Good quality of materials
  • Complementary to subject building
  • Well maintained
  • Improvement to "streetscene"

234 In general the quality of hard landscaping tended to be low and in the case of the industrial and retail sectors actually detracted from the quality of the subject building. Only the office sector was dominated by projects with good quality hard landscaping. Table 4.11A below demonstrates this:

Elements that constitute good design in hard landscaping:

  – Improves the local "streetscene"
  – Strong visual impact
  – Good quality materials and well maintained
  – Meets functional needs

Table 4.10 – Quality of design: Building quality						
Project Type	0	1	2	3	4	All
Offices	0	0	1	4	5	10
Industrial	0	1	2	7	1	11
Retail	0	1	2	2	1	6
Hotels	0	0	0	2	1	3
Housing	0	3	1	1	1	6
All	0	5	6	16	9	36

Table 4.11A – Quality of design: Hard landscaping							
Project Type	0	1	2	3	4	N/A	All
Offices	0	0	1	3	2	4	10
Industrial	2	2	3	1	2	1	11
Retail	1	2	0	1	1	1	6
Hotels	0	0	1	0	0	2	3
Housing	2	1	1	1	0	1	6
All	5	5	6	6	5	9	36

Soft Landscaping

235 In 22 out of 36 cases the project included an element of soft landscaping. Quality in this element was measured in terms of:

- Strong visual impact
- Complementary to the subject building and hard landscaping
- Successful planting regimes and well maintained
- Improvement to "street scene"

236 In general the quality of soft landscaping tended to be slightly lower than general building quality. Nevertheless 14 out of 22 projects had either good or excellent soft landscaping. Table 4.11B below demonstrates the variation in quality over different use types.

237 Our findings demonstrate that in the 4 cases out of 10 where office projects had soft landscaping it was either very good or of an excellent standard.

238 In 10 cases out of a total of 11 industrial schemes included an element of landscaping. There was, however, an enormous range in quality with two deemed to be excellent (Birmingham, IMI, Holford and Southwark, Priter Way Railway Arches) and three being deemed poor (Birmingham, Garrison Lane; Birmingham, Startpoint Industrial Units; Nottingham, Southglade Park).

239 The most surprising finding was that the quality of soft landscaping in the housing projects was generally of a poor standard in 3 out of 5 cases.

240 In general projects had better quality hard and soft landscaping where the obligation to maintain was clearly defined. Whilst good design and materials are important contributors to overall quality the regularity of maintenance is essential. The presence of litter and poorly maintained trees and shrubs is a major detractor.

Pollution

241 Although a large number of City Grant schemes have dealt with the removal of dereliction and contamination, in our sample only Beechdale Engineering, Nottingham and Hartlepool Business Park were considered to have dealt with pollution. In the former case local residents suffered from noise pollution which led to the pressure to relocate to the urban fringe in order to extend the daily operating period and improve productivity of machinery. In the latter case the site was contaminated.

Summary of site level changes

242 The schemes which produced the greatest environmental impact as a result of changes to their site were relatively large with high visibility and which involved the re-using of formerly derelict sites. Table 4.12 below summarises our assessment of site changes.

AREA LEVEL CHANGES

Introduction

243 Although the latest City Grant guidance notes set out the environmental objectives the policy aims to achieve, earlier guidance was not so clear. At the grant appraisal stage only 6 out of 36 projects were set objectives that involved the scheme bringing about area change. This does not imply that environmental issues were not considered, simply that they were not made specific in the appraisal case paper (this will be discussed further under recommendations).

244 The most obvious is Stoney Street, Nottingham which involved the development of a multi-storey car park which was seen as removing a constraint to the regeneration of the Lace Market Conservation Area.

Table 4.11B – Quality of design: Soft landscaping							
Project Type	0	1	2	3	4	N/A	All
Offices	0	0	0	2	2	6	10
Industrial	3	0	4	1	2	1	11
Retail	1	1	0	1	0	3	6
Hotels	0	0	0	0	0	3	3
Housing	3	0	0	2	0	1	6
All	7	1	4	6	4	14	36

Table 4.12 – Summary of site changes

	Site Area	Floorspace developed	Overall passing visibility	Overlooking dwellings	Prominence	Removal of dereliction	Conservation	Reduction of detractors	Increased usage of site	Quality of design	Traffic and parking	Pollution
OFFICES												
Birmingham, 3–5 St Paul's Square	1	1	4	4	2	4	4	2	5	3	−3	0
Birmingham, Snowhill Station	2	2	5	0	4	0	0	2	3	4	0	0
Leicester, Arnhem House	1	3	4	2	5	1	0	2	3	3	−1	0
Manchester, Albion House	1	2	4	0	4	4	4	5	5	4	−1	0
Newcastle, 43/49 Grey Street	1	2	4	0	3	4	4	1	4	4	0	0
Nottingham, Newcastle House	2	3	4	3	2	3	5	2	5	3	0	0
Nottingham, Stoney Street (also included car park development)	2	3	3	3	2	0	0	0	3	3	4	0
Oldham, Union Street	2	2	4	1	1	3	0	2	4	4	0	0
Sheffield, Huttons Buildings	1	2	4	1	3	1	2	1	4	2	0	0
Southwark, Archbishop Temple Business Units	1	2	3	5	3	1	2	0	5	3	0	0
INDUSTRIAL												
Birmingham, Garrison Lane	3	3	3	4	2	5	0	4	5	2	0	0
Birmingham, IMI Holford Park	5	5	3	5	4	4	0	1	5	4	0	0
Birmingham, Newhall Hill	2	2	2	0	3	2	3	2	5	2	0	0
Birmingham, Startpoint Industrial Units	3	3	3	4	2	3	0	3	5	1	0	0
Boldon Business Park	5	4	1	3	1	0	0	0	5	2	0	0
Hartlepool, Hartlepool Business Park	3	4	2	0	1	5	0	0	5	2	0	0
Nottingham, Beechdale Engineering	4	3	1	0	1	0	0	0	5	3	0	4
Nottingham, Southglade Park	5	4	3	5	2	2	0	2	3	2	0	0
Oldham, MCM Ltd	2	1	3	3	1	0	0	2	5	1	0	0

continued

Table 4.12 continued – Summary of site changes

	Site area and floorspace	Overall passing visibility	Overlooking dwellings	Prominence	Removal of dereliction	Increased usage of site	Quality of design	Conservation	Traffic and parking and pollution
Oldham, Stamford Mill	3	3	2	3	1	3	0	0	0
Southwark, Prier Way Arches	3	3	3	5	3	5	2	0	0
RETAIL									
Birmingham, One Stop, Perry Bar	5	5	4	5	4	4	0	3	0
Bolton, Bark Street	3	4	5	0	4	4	4	4	0
Gateshead, Felling Town Centre	2	3	4	3	3	4	1	4	0
Hull, Bransholme North	3	2	3	5	2	0	0	0	0
Middlesbrough, Zetland Road (also included office development)	1	2	5	0	3	4	2	0	0
South Shields, Catherine Street	2	1	4	0	3	3	0	0	0
HOTELS									
Birmingham, Paradise Circus (also included office development)	3	5	5	0	4	0	0	2	0
Manchester, Midland Hotel	2	5	5	3	4	1	4	4	0
Nottingham, Rutland Square Hotel	1	4	2	3	1	4	2	0	0
HOUSING									
Birmingham, The Parade	3	2	4	0	3	0	0	0	0
Hull, Coltman Street	3	3	3	5	2	3	2	0	0
Hull, Courtauld's Warehouse (also included retail development)	2	2	4	4	4	2	4	0	0
Nottingham, Mundella Court	3	3	3	4	1	3	0	0	0
Nottingham, Southglade Park	5	4	3	5	2	2	0	0	0
Oldham, Bank Top Mill	4	4	2	5	1	3	0	0	0

Notes: The scores for the following characteristics are in accordance with earlier tables. The values are as follows:

Site area and floorspace (see table 4.1)
1 = small   5 = large
Overall passing visibility (see table 4.3)
Overlooking dwellings (see table 4.4)
Prominence (see table 4.5)

Removal of dereliction (see table 4.6)
Increased usage of site (see table 4.11)
Quality of design (see table 4.12C)

Conservation
In-keeping with the area   = 1
Retention of an old building   = 2
Within a Conservation Area   = 3
Grade 2 or 2* Listed Building   = 4

Traffic and parking and pollution
Worsening   = Negative score
No change   = 0
Slight improvement   = 1

Moderate improvement   = 2
Significant improvement = 3
Major improvement   = 4

245 Three projects were seen as assisting existing area regeneration strategies, (Courtauld's Warehouse, Hull; Bark Street, Bolton and Midland Hotel, Manchester).

246 In the case of Beechdale Engineering, Nottingham the objective was to remove a bad neighbour and to enhance the residential neighbourhood surrounding the old factory site.

247 Finally in the case of Paradise Circus, Birmingham the site was a relic from the Local Authority Master Plan era and the project was seen to have benefits of unifying the area in urban design terms.

248 We identified area changes since the start of the individual survey schemes from our discussions with Local Authority officers, estate agents and where appropriate the project developer. This gave us an adequate background from which to comment on broad area changes.

249 Substantially more difficult however, is the teasing out of the impact or contribution of the scheme to broader area changes. A rigorous attempt has been made to avoid the trap of identifying area change that has taken place following a scheme's completion and simply attributing those changes to the scheme. Other potential determinants of area change which we have identified across the sample have included.

- Signs of up-lift in the area before and after the scheme
- The type and timing of other public sector funded projects in the area
- Local property market changes
- Local economic changes

250 The project sample is also drawn from those that were approved between December 1982 and December 1989. As a result some schemes have had a longer period to be assimilated within the market than others and in turn have had longer to impact on an area.

Overall Area Changes

251 We have defined the overall area change as all changes in the surrounding area beyond the boundary of the project. The appropriate area over which to estimate area change varies according to the size and type of project and indeed its impact. In all cases the maximum extent of change that we have considered is 0.5km from the outer boundary of the project.

Private Sector Investment

252 In nearly all of the areas surrounding the sample projects (31 out of 36) there was indication of private sector investment. Ten of the thirty-six projects are in areas that have experienced significant increase in private sector investment. Two areas (Birmingham, 3–5 St Pauls Square and Hull, Coltman Street) have changed dramatically. No clear pattern emerges regarding the influence of locality or type of project however, it is clear that earlier projects have higher levels of private sector investment than more recently completed schemes.

Detractors

253 The level of detractors in the surrounding neighbourhood was generally found not to have changed significantly. Twelve projects are in areas where there is not discernable change and nineteen projects are in areas where there has been a slight reduction in detractors. Our analysis was entirely subjective; no statistics on vandalism, crime or fly tipping were obtained.

254 Only in the cases of 3–5 St Paul's Square, Birmingham; Albion House, Manchester and Coltman Street, Hull were there major improvements at an area level.

Levels of Economic Activity and New Activities/ Facilities

255 Economic activity was gauged from a subjective assessment of changes in the stock of accommodation, occupancy/vacancy levels and change of use in the area. This subjective assessment was supported by floorspace and local authority planning data, where available.

256 New activities or facilities were identified from a subjective assessment of the age of facilities. This analysis was supported by discussions with Local Authority officers and local property agents.

257 Not surprisingly, a strong association between levels of private sector investment and levels of economic activity and addition to or improvement of activities/ facilities was identified. The only main exception to this pattern is Coltman Street, Hull where there has been a very significant increase in private sector investment and little change to either levels of economic activity or to new activities/facilities. All of the private sector investment in this instance was in the form of housing.

258 Elsewhere investment has intended to be in a mixture of land uses which in turn has promoted a localised increase in the level of economic activity, the range of types of activities and the number and range of facilities.

259 In several instances the overall level of economic activity has risen rather more than the number of new activities. Three factors accounted for this:

- All of the areas benefitted from improvements to the national economy which increased economic activity in existing firms,
- Several of the schemes were in areas dominated by or suited to a particular use and thus changes added "more of the same".
- In the case of city centre schemes a full range of activities and facilities was already present.

Traffic and Parking

260 Nineteen of the projects are in areas where no perceptible change to traffic or parking has occurred. Of the remaining seventeen congestion and/or car parking worsened in eight cases, and improved in eleven cases.

261 Few schemes are considered to have had anything other than a negligible effect on traffic and car parking at the site level. Most schemes provided sufficient car parking to meet the needs of the project and considered to have had a marginal effect on traffic generation in the area.

262 Five projects produced a measurable net overall benefit to the surrounding area. In three out of five cases these were retail schemes (One Stop, Birmingham; Felling Town Centre, Gateshead and Bark Street Bolton). The other two schemes included were hotel and office (Paradise Circus, Birmingham) and primarily a multi-storey car park development (with an office component) at Storey Street, Nottingham which serves the Lace Market regeneration area.

263 Three schemes produced a net disbenefit all of which were office projects (Albion House, Manchester; Arnhem House, Leicester and 3–5 St Paul's Square, Birmingham).

Pollution

264 The only project to be associated with a change in pollution is Beechdale Engineering Ltd, Nottingham. The adjacent residential area has experienced a reduction in noise pollution as a result of the move.

265 IMI PLC's operations adjacent to IMI Holford in Birmingham have changed since the project began but changes in pollution levels have not been identified.

Area Impact (area changes attributable to the sample projects)

266 Nearly all of the projects were found to be situated in locations where area changes have taken place and where there has been an overall uplift. However, because of the buoyant state of the property market in the second half of the 1980s and other public sector investment in the areas it is impossible to determine with any certainty how much, if any, of the change can be attributed to the projects.

267 Our assessment is that nine projects probably contributed to significant area change. Without exception these were developed in the mid 80s and are amongst the earliest approved schemes. They are:

- Birmingham, 3–5 St Paul's Square
- Nottingham, Stoney Street
- Nottingham, Beechdale Engineering
- Bolton, Bark Street
- Manchester, Midland Hotel
- Birmingham, The Parade
- Hull, Coltman Street
- Hull, Courtauld's Warehouse
- South Shields, Catherine Street

268 Six other projects probably had some influence, thought it may have been slight:

- Nottingham, Newcastle House
- Boldon, Boldon Business Park
- Birmingham, One Stop, Perry Bar
- Gateshead, Felling Town Centre
- Nottingham, Rutland Square

269 It is noteworthy that eleven out of the fifteen schemes listed above involved a strongly pro-active Local Authority involvement with at least ten involving the use of other Urban Programme resources for adjacent projects.

CONCLUSIONS

270 Whilst the majority of schemes (28 out of 36) were not set specific environmentally based objectives in the appraisal case papers, all of the projects in the sample have contributed to the improvement of the site and in turn to the improvement of the area. While we are aware that appraisers do reflect the environmental benefits in their assessment of a project more formal and explicit objectives would allow more straight forward evaluation and ensure that the appropriate weight is applied to environmental benefits.

271 Schemes developing prominent derelict or vacant sites on main road frontages contributed most to significant overall environmental uplift.

272 A number of the projects contributed to wider area environmental improvements, most significantly as part of wider public sector strategies and investment programmes.

273 High quality schemes may well be particularly effective in assisting area regeneration, by contributing to changing the image of an area and by achieving a high rental which sets a marker for subsequent developments in the locality.

274 Our analysis clearly shows that the removal of dereliction and its replacement with high quality accommodation has a significant demonstration effect in encouraging further economic activity. While we are aware that this is considered by appraisers we believe that this should be made explicit at appraisal and given sufficient weight to encourage projects even where the traditional value for money terms are not met. Formal assessment criteria and weighting in the case papers would help to ensure this is encouraged.

5 Social and community impact

SOCIAL OBJECTIVES AND POTENTIAL BENEFITS

275   The Urban Development Grant regime sought to achieve, *inter alia*, social objectives. The relevant Guidance Notes specifically stated that projects ". . . should make a demonstrable contribution to meeting the special social needs of inner urban areas". As a result, the degree to which social needs were to be tackled was an important criterion in the appraisal of Urban Development Grant applications.

276   On the other hand, City Grant objectives have not, until very recently, included any explicit reference to social needs. The original Guidance Notes, dating back to 1988, had remained unaltered through to January 1992. Now, a wider range of objectives are associated with City Grant including social benefits.

277   To an extent, City Grant appraisals have considered social objectives at least in terms of the provision of jobs. Impact on the community can subsequently be addressed by identifying the extent to which the new jobs created directly benefitted local people.

Methodology

278   Although, the revised Guidance Notes for City Grant applicants only refers to an increase in the ". . . choice of facilities available in the area", a variety of alternative criteria exist against which each project can be scored.

279   Subjective assessments have been made of the level of benefit attributable to each project ranging from zero benefit (score 0) to high benefit (score 3) – for example, see Table 5.1. The scores were arrived at following a visit to each site and subsequent discussions with local authority officials and local property agents.

280   "Jobs for local people", a criterion relevant only to commercial and industrial schemes, has been assessed quantitatively as follows;

Level of benefit	% of jobs for local people
3	75+
2	25–75
1	0–25
0	0

281   Housing and non-housing schemes have been separately analysed given the relevance of certain criteria to one category or the other.

282   The social benefits provided by both housing and non-housing schemes are:

- Removal of hazard
- Removal of visual disamenity or pollutant
- Increase in the number of residents or workers, thereby increasing the demand for local facilities and services (support for existing facilities/services).

283   Further, potential benefits associated with housing schemes are;

- Housing for local residents (increased availability and/or affordability).
- Adding to the social mix (new social groups).

284   To a greater or lesser degree, the non-housing schemes offered the following benefits;

- Jobs for local residents.
- Additional facilities for local residents or workers.

285   While the word "local" is synonymous with the Inner Area in the above context, there are difficulties in determining, for example, the precise proportion of employees resident within the Inner Area.

HOUSING SCHEMES

286 The objectives of housing schemes tend to be primarily environmental and social. The two main social rationales for housing schemes are:

- To bring new economically active residents into the area, adding to income and expenditure in the area and to the social mix.
- To provide affordable homes (generally for owner occupation) for inner city residents, to enable them to improve their housing conditions while remaining in the area.

287 Table 5.1 shows the analysis of housing schemes against the relevant set of criteria.

288 Four of the six schemes (Southglade Park, Nottingham, Bank Top Mill, Oldham, Mundella Court, Nottingham and Courtaulds Warehouse, Hull) required grant support primarily because of either building or ground constraints. The main objective was the re-use of a difficult site rather than addressing a social objective.

289 All schemes added to the amount of housing choice in the Inner Area and by contributing to the amount of housing stock (especially for first time buyers) and increasing the residential population in the Inner Area contributed to maintaining (or enhancing) the range and/or quality of services and facilities. They therefore indirectly benefit existing residents. With the exception of Mundella Court, Nottingham, the sale price of dwellings was lower than the average price of other new dwellings in the respective Inner Areas, not because City Grant enabled developers to undercut the market but because City Grant aided houses were generally smaller or on less attractive sites.

290 Bank Top Mill, Oldham and Southglade Park, Nottingham, both provide over 100 affordable homes for people from the surrounding areas wishing to move up the housing ladder. The majority of the demand for houses in both of the schemes is perceived to be local.

291 The dwellings provided by the Mundella Court, Nottingham scheme are approximately twice the price of adjacent dwellings. It is consequently assumed that new residents and different social groups will have been attracted to the scheme adding to the social mix of the Inner Area.

292 The Parade, Birmingham, scheme provides low cost houses for rent, and associated (but non-UDG funded) elements of the scheme provided social and community facilities which include a day care centre and creche.

293 The Coltman Street, Hull, scheme has attracted owner occupiers to the street where dwellings were previously mainly private rented, with many in multiple occupancy. The scheme has also provided affordable houses for Inner Area residents.

	New Social Groups	Increased availability/ affordability	Removal of hazard	Removal of visual disamenity or pollutant	Support for existing facilities/ services
Table 5.1 – Social and community impacts – Housing schemes					
Birmingham, The Parade	1	3	0	0	2
Hull, Coltman Street	2	2	2	3	3
Hull, Courtauld's Warehouse	2	1	1	1	1
Nottingham, Mundella Court	3	0	2	1	1
Nottingham, Southglade Park	1–2	1	1	2	3
Oldham, Bank Top Mill	1	1	2	3	3

Level of benefit
3 = High
2 = Medium
1 = Low
0 = Zero

COMMERCIAL AND INDUSTRIAL SCHEMES

294 The creation of jobs is assumed to be the key objective of grant assistance for commercial and industrial schemes. On a number of occasions, schemes were also expected to produce significant environmental benefits.

295 The potential social benefits of commercial and industrial schemes can be summarised under a number of headings. The relative impact of projects in terms of these variables is summarised in Table 5.2.

296 The provision of jobs for local people is assessed based on information from the survey of occupants. The quality of information from scheme occupants regarding where their employees live was variable and there is some element of subjectivity in the assessment. The provision of new facilities is assessed on the basis of likely benefits to local residents and workers.

New Jobs for Local People

297 Few schemes have produced a significant number of net additional jobs for those from within the Inner Area. The majority of schemes produced a low level of net additional jobs, that is less than 25%, for local people when displacement (in its various forms) is taken into account (see Chapter 3).

298 Only one scheme, Beechdale Engineering, Nottingham, resulted in the provision of a relatively high number of such jobs. The circumstances are somewhat unusual in that the jobs were in fact internal transfers yet were not disregarded as displacement. Had the company not relocated to the urban fringe, it is believed that it would have either closed down or moved to an alternative location outside the Inner Area.

299 Several schemes such as Albion House, Manchester, Hartlepool Business Park and Oldham MCM produced no net additional jobs for local people. These comprise both office and industrial developments but beyond that there is no discernable pattern.

Provision of New Facilities and Services

300 The schemes attracting the highest scores for the provision of new facilities and services tend to be retail developments. Bransholme North, Hull, a new shopping centre in a peripheral housing scheme, is a very significant development in terms of the provision of a new facility creating social and community benefits. Prior to its development, residents were required to travel some distance for the majority of their convenience shopping. Both this scheme and Felling Town Centre created a new focus of social activity. In the face of a dispersal of retailing activity and a general run down in the condition of the former High Street outlets, the Felling Town Centre scheme may be considered a bold attempt to reinstate the High Street as the principal retailing destination. The retail schemes in Bolton, Birmingham and South Tyneside also delivered specific social and community benefits to residents and workers in their respective areas. Beyond being purely retail facilities, some developments offer eating and other recreational facilities available to all members of the public. At Bolton, the retail development incorporated the refurbishment of an adjoining eighteenth century market hall. The main entrance to the centre is now via the operational market hall, where the character of the old market has survived and operators are principally local traders.

301 To a degree, the leisure facilities (hotels) also offer non-employment benefits to residents and workers. The extent, however, to which local residents and workers actually make use of the public bars and restaurants is difficult to determine.

302 A number of schemes provide surface level or multi-storey car parking facilities. Use of such car parks is not restricted to users of the associated retail outlets at, for example, Felling and Bolton. At Storey Street, Nottingham, the prime objective was to provide a multi-storey car park to alleviate the parking difficulties in the immediate area.

303 A creche was provided at Archbishop Temple Units, Southwark. The facility is effectively open to the public rather than being restricted to employees housed in the business units. Despite this, the overall score attributed to the scheme is low since the business units offer no additional facilities or services to local residents or workers.

Support for Existing Facilities and Services

304 At a basic level, an increase in the number of workers or residents within an area is likely to result in a related increase in the demand for existing facilities and services or perhaps for new support facilities and services. Following the development of the Rutland Square Hotel in Nottingham, premises on the other side of the square were converted into function rooms and conference facilities available to residents of the inner area amongst others. Induced development of this nature is discussed more fully in Chapter 2. In Manchester, it is believed that the Midland Hotel and Albion House have successfully complemented the nearby G-MEX exhibition centre.

305 It is reasonable to assume that the provision of public car parking, although related to specific

schemes, also lends support to surrounding facilities and services by enabling additional car-borne shoppers to visit the area. This is particularly so in relation to inner city locations with parking difficulties such as Bark Street, Bolton.

Removal of Hazard

306 Only 3 out of the 30 schemes investigated involved the removal of a hazard. The hazards were buildings in various states of disrepair, some close to collapse. In Middlesbrough, East Mercia Developments as part of the company's comprehensive office and retail development scheme, undertook the rebuilding of a seriously fire-damaged listed Victorian building within a Conservation Area. In the absence of the development, it is likely that the building would have been demolished by the local authority. Albion House in Manchester was in a derelict state prior to redevelopment of this Grade 2 listed building. Again, it is believed that the premises would have been demolished if Inner City Enterprises plc had not undertaken its redevelopment. Finally, Priter Way Arches, Southwark were in a dangerous condition and accessible to the public prior to redevelopment.

307 While the site of Hartlepool Business Park had formerly been used as a tip by BSC, it would be wrong to claim that the materials on the site actually constituted a hazard to the local population.

Removal of Disamenity or pollutant

308 Several schemes partly or fully removed a visual disamenity. The Beechdale Engineering, Nottingham, scheme in particular merits a high score since it resulted in the relocation of a heavy industrial plant from the Inner Area to the urban fringe. The previous site was in a largely residential area of Nottingham. Other than this scheme, none resulted in the removal of a pollutant. There is generally a strong correlation between those schemes scoring high in terms of removal of hazard and removal of disamenity where the hazard refers to the condition of a building. At Felling, while the former terraced shops were not classified as "hazards", they were typically in poor condition. Their removal therefore constitutes a significant improvement in terms of visual amenity.

CONCLUSIONS

309 In appraisal papers benefits are typically expressed in terms of job creation (permanent and construction) and housing provision. On occasion, explicit reference is made to projected environmental benefits. However, rarely is any explicit mention made of social and community benefits. Again we are aware that these issues are considered by appraisers, however, we believe that specific reference to these benefits in the case paper would enable evaluation and ensure consistency and due weight is given.

310 Only a small percentage of the jobs estimated at appraisal stage were found to be held by resident of the inner area. Our analysis did however reveal that specific sectors created more local jobs than others. City Grant is however a demand led policy and does not therefore encourage or discourage specific types of development or influence who and where occupiers source their employment.

311 As regards housing schemes, although the appraisal process does consider social and community impacts it does not specify the precise ways nor the extent to which such schemes might benefit the local area. Accordingly, the social benefits achieved cannot be measured against any set targets. Having said that, where the objective has been to vary the tenure and/ or the cost of accommodation and therefore encourage economically active people to remain or move into the area, this objective appears to have been met.

312 Despite the general lack of any reference to social and community benefits in appraisal papers, some schemes have demonstrated tangible benefits. Particularly high scores in all of our categories are associated with three retail schemes because shopping itself is widely accepted as being, in part, a social activity. These schemes have added to an existing shopping hierarchy but also provided associated leisure or "non-core" facilities (for example restaurants or food court, market hall, landscaped communal areas).

313 To a limited extent, the social objective of reducing social disamenity has been tackled in the appraisal process in terms of being an environmental objective. For example, it was clearly stated that one projected benefit resulting from the redevelopment of Felling High Street was a "considerable" gain to the environment. Similarly, the prevention of fly-tipping through the active redevelopment of Priter Way Arches, Southwark, was noted as an anticipated environmental benefit which also significantly improved the visual amenity of the area.

314 We have considered whether social and community benefits might have been enhanced by stipulating that, as a condition of the offer of grant, the relevant development should house a given proportion (or range) of inner city employees. While this may appear a simple and direct mechanism to ensure inner city developments benefit local employees, we believe it unworkable for the following principal reasons:

- where a development comprises something new to the inner area or perhaps a new "product" entirely, the supply of labour with the requisite skills for the targeted occupiers may be somewhat restricted in the inner area.
- developers would be less interested if they were expected to market their projects subject to such special conditions.
- there would be a significant administrative burden imposed on occupiers if there was imposed anything other than a one-off initial obligation to house a certain number of inner city employees.

6 Value for money

315 In this chapter we set out summary indicators of 'value for money' in terms of grant effectiveness (gross and net outputs) and efficiency (the ratio of inputs to outputs) for each project in the sample.

CALCULATION OF NET GRANT INPUT

316 In 21 out of 36 schemes the full amount of grant approved at application stage has been taken up by the developer and has been adopted as the actual net input.

317 In the remainder of the sample the net grant awarded falls short of the actual approved. This is for the following reasons:

318 Firstly, each grant agreement (with the exception of some of the earliest projects) contains a clawback clause which enables DoE to recover 50% of 'surplus value' above that projected in the original application. Claw-back has been received on seven of the sampled projects to date.

319 Secondly, grant is paid on 'allowable costs' incurred by the developer. In the case of another seven projects the actual costs fell short of those projected in the application. As a result the full grant amount was not released to the developer.

320 Finally in the case of Southglade Park, Nottingham (Housing) the developer sold the development prior to completion to a competitor which resulted in the termination of the grant agreement and the cessation of grant payments.

321 Broadly, however the figures provided in Table 6.1 provide an accurate account of the level of public sector input. In many cases projects still have unexpired clawback clauses which may, in time reduce the net grant award. In the following tables we have used the definitions below:

- Project cost: contained in appraisal papers
- Actual costs: derived from developer, if not obtained then projected costs are adopted as actual
- Projected value: contained in appraisal papers
- Actual value: derived from developer:
  - if sold then sales proceeds are actual values

  - if retained the developers view of value at the time of interview
  - if not derived from developer then projected value used as actual value

PRIVATE SECTOR INVESTMENT

322 One of the key objectives of City Grant and its predecessors has been to lever additional private sector investment into the inner city. We have therefore checked whether the projects were indeed additional and what gearing ratio they actually achieved.

323 The additionality of the project investment was discussed in Chapter 2. We looked at deadweight (projects that would have happened anyway) and displacement (projects which might have crowded out other investments.) We found only one project (Grey St Newcastle) which with hindsight could have eventually proceeded unaided but concluded that even in this case there was only limited deadweight as the project would not have proceeded at the time without grant. We found equally little sign of grant aided projects displacing other investment. Thus for the purpose of calculating efficiency indicators (grant per job and per house) we have treated all the *projects* (but not necessarily their outputs) as additional.

Gearing Ratio

324 Gearing or leverage is defined as the ratio of grant to private sector investment. As grant makes up the difference between costs and value then the latter element represents the level of private sector investment in the project. It will be seen in Table 6.1 that, as would be expected, outturn costs and values sometimes differ from those projected at the time of the grant appraisal. Where the values change, and as a result some of the grant is clawed back, the outturn gearing will also differ from the projection. This effect can be seen in Table 6.2.

325 When a completed development has been sold we have been able to calculate the outturn gearing ratio by dividing the sale proceeds by the net grant paid. Where, as in 19 of the 36 projects, developments were retained by the developers we asked them to

Table 6.1 – Value for Money: grant, costs and value

Project Name	Grant approved £	Net Grant awarded £	Grant recovered by DoE	Costs (including profit)		Value	
				Projected £	Actual £	Projected £	Actual £
OFFICES							
Birmingham, 3–5 St Paul's Square	102,000	102,000	0%	364,000	423,000	262,000	262,000 ◄
Birmingham, Snowhill Station	200,000	179,883	10%	5,949,798	5,949,798	5,749,798	5,749,798
Leicester, Arnhem House	708,200	705,612	0%	6,787,275	6,060,000	6,079,075	6,400,000
Manchester, Albion House	301,000	301,000	0%	1,479,400	2,243,000	1,178,400	2,250,000 ►
Newcastle, 43/49 Grey Street	487,500	280,148	43%	4,147,500	3,666,000 ■	3,660,000	3,660,000 ◄
Nottingham, Newcastle House	735,000	498,962	32%	4,449,200	4,317,350	3,714,200	4,171,220
Nottingham, Stoney Street	940,000	940,000	0%	3,380,000	3,380,000 ■	2,440,000	2,440,000 ◄
Oldham, Union Street	644,000	644,000	0%	1,811,000	1,824,000	1,167,000	1,200,000
Sheffield, Huttons	269,750	238,646	12%	1,789,891	1,483,165 ■	1,520,141	1,370,000
Southwark, Abp T Business Units	500,000	500,000 ▢	0%	4,098,560	4,985,000	3,598,560	2,560,000 ►
INDUSTRIAL							
Birmingham, Garrison Lane	570,000	570,000 ▢	0%	3,476,000	3,950,000	2,906,000	3,000,000 ►
Birmingham, IMI Holford Park	5,685,000	4,096,000	28%	22,380,000	22,556,000 ■	16,695,000	16,695,000 ◄
Birmingham, Newhall Hill	70,000	70,000	0%	372,815	372,815 ■	302,815	302,815 ◄
Birmingham, Startpoint Industrial Units	283,000	283,000 ▢	0%	1,133,000	1,100,000	850,000	1,625,000 ►
Boldon Business Park	1,230,940	1,230,940	0%	3,702,734	3,624,955 ■	2,471,794	2,471,794 ◄
Hartlepool, Hartlepool Business Park	634,600	634,600	0%	4,574,000	3,939,400 ■	3,939,400	3,939,400 ◄
Nottingham, Beechdale Engineering	1,055,000	1,055,000	0%	5,054,000	5,054,000	3,999,000	3,999,000 ◄
Nottingham, Southglade Park	386,385	357,000	2%	1,563,385	1,565,000 ■	1,200,000	1,200,000 ◄
Oldham, MCM Ltd	31,000	31,000	0%	135,000	137,700	104,000	104,000 ◄
Oldham, Stamford Mill	224,725	224,725	0%	746,225	798,460	521,500	1,269,000

continued

Project Name	Grant approved £	Net Grant awarded £	Grant recovered by DoE	Costs (including profit)		Value	
				Projected £	Actual £	Projected £	Actual £
Table 6.1 continued – Value for Money: grant, costs and value							
Southwark, Priter Way Arches	525,000	477,451 ◘	9%	3,025,000	2,825,000	2,500,000	2,100,000 ►
RETAIL							
Birmingham, One Stop, Perry Bar	2,620,000	2,620,000 ◘	0%	21,684,164	15,300,600	19,064,164	19,064,164 ◄
Bolton, Bark Street	4,500,000	4,235,000	6%	37,540,000	39,932,720	33,040,000	34,000,000 ►
Gateshead, Felling Town Centre	575,000	575,000	0%	2,777,000	2,806,949	2,202,000	2,035,957
Hull, Bransholme North	330,000	277,465	16%	985,000	1,115,000	655,000	805,000
Middlesbrough, Zetland Road (also included office development)	661,000	661,000 ◘	0%	3,100,760	2,439,760 ■	2,439,760	2,439,760 ◄
South Shields, Catherine Street	74,000	74,000	0%	698,000	770,826	624,000	624,000 ◄
HOTELS							
Birmingham, Paradise Circus (also included office development)	4,680,550	4,680,550	0%	10,380,000	11,980,000	5,699,450	5,700,000 ◄
Manchester, Midland Hotel	2,200,000	2,200,000	0%	13,037,000	12,400,000	10,837,000	10,837,000 ◄
Nottingham, Rutland Square Hotel	738,000	738,000 ◘	0%	3,216,000	4,819,843	2,478,000	5,000,000 ►
HOUSING							
Birmingham, The Parade	543,000	531,099	2%	1,719,338	2,451,000	1,176,338	1,176,338 ◄
Hull, Coltman Street	952,020	952,020	0%	2,630,269	2,630,269 ■	1,678,249	1,678,249 ◄
Hull, Courtauld's Warehouse (also included retail development)	244,000	229,000	6%	856,000	862,000	612,000	636,000
Nottingham, Mundella Court	216,400	0	100%	2,671,400	2,671,400	2,455,000	2,455,000 ◄
Nottingham, Southglade Park	536,615	189,096	65%	6,493,000	6,493,000 ■	5,954,000	2,977,000
Oldham, Bank Top Mill	390,570	50,000 ◘	87%	3,631,968	3,631,968 ■	3,241,398	4,440,666

Note: ◘   Net grant award based on the latest details of grant award and claw-back.

    ■   The developer has not provided actual costs. Appraised costs have been applied.

Where the developer has not sold the completed development the actual value is based on one of two assumptions.

    ►   Estimate of value provided by developer in absence of total sales proceeds.

    ◄   The projected sales value is used as the actual value.

Table 6.2 – Ratio of net public expenditure to private (gearing)				
	Projected		Actual	
	Ratio (1:)	%	Ratio (1:)	%
OFFICES				
Birmingham, 3–5 St Paul's Square	2.6	38.9%	2.6	38.9%
Birmingham, Snowhill Station	28.7	3.5%	32.0	3.1%
Leicester, Arnhem House	8.6	11.6%	9.0	11.1%
Manchester, Albion House	3.9	25.6%	7.5	13.4%
Newcastle, 43/49 Grey Street	7.5	13.3%	13.1	7.7%
Nottingham, Newcastle House	5.1	19.6%	8.4	12.0%
Nottingham, Stoney Street	2.6	38.5%	2.6	38.5%
Oldham, Union Street	1.8	55.6%	1.9	53.7%
Sheffield, Huttons	5.6	17.9%	5.7	17.4%
Southwark, Archbishop Temple Business Units	7.2	13.9%	5.1	19.5%
INDUSTRIAL				
Birmingham, Garrison Lane	5.1	19.6%	5.3	18.9%
Birmingham, IMI Holdford Park	2.9	34.1%	4.1	24.5%
Birmingham, Newhall Hill	4.3	23.1%	4.3	23.1%
Birmingham, Startpoint Industrial Units	3.0	33.3%	5.7	17.4%
Boldon Business Park	2.0	49.8%	2.0	49.8%
Hartlepool, Hartlepool Business Park	6.2	16.1%	6.2	16.1%
Nottingham, Beechdale Engineering	3.8	26.4%	3.8	26.4%
Nottingham, Southglade Park	3.3	30.3%	3.4	29.8%
Oldham, MCM Ltd	3.4	29.8%	3.4	29.8%
Oldham, Stamford Mill	2.3	43.5%	5.6	17.7%
Southwark, Priter Way Arches	4.8	20.8%	4.4	22.7%
RETAIL				
Birmingham, One Stop, Perry Bar	7.3	13.7%	7.3	13.7%
Bolton, Bark Street	7.3	13.2%	8.0	12.5%
Gateshead, Felling Town Centre	3.8	26.3%	3.5	28.2%
Hull, Bransholme North	2.0	50.0%	2.9	34.5%
Middlesbrough, Zetland Road (also included office development)	3.7	27.1%	2.7	37.3%
South Shields, Catherine Street	8.4	11.9%	8.4	11.9%

continued

51

Table 6.2 continued – Ratio of net public expenditure to private (gearing)				
	Projected		Actual	
	Ratio (1:)	%	Ratio (1:)	%
HOTELS				
Birmingham, Paradise Circus (also included office development)	1.2	82.1%	1.2	82.1%
Manchester, Midland Hotel	4.9	20.3%	4.9	20.3%
Nottingham, Rutland Square Hotel	5.3	18.9%	6.8	14.8%
HOUSING				
Birmingham, The Parade	2.2	46.2%	2.2	45.1%
Hull, Coltman Street	1.8	56.7%	1.8	56.7%
Hull, Courtauld's Warehouse (also included retail development)	2.5	38.4%	2.8	36.0%
Nottingham, Mudella Court	11.3	8.8%	N/A	Grant repaid
Nottingham, Southglade Park	11.1	9.0%	15.7	6.4%
Oldham, Bank Top Mill	8.3	12.0%	88.8	1.1%

Note:

The percentage figures express the relationship between the net amount of public expenditure after clawback in a project to that invested by the private sector. If a project has a 1:1 gearing ratio then the percentage that private sector investment represents in relation to the public sector contribution will be 100%.

Table 6.2B – Comparative analysis by use type				
Use Type	Projected		Actual	
	Ratio (1:)	%	Ratio (1:)	%
Offices	6.0	16.3%	6.8	14.6%
Industrial	3.3	29.1%	4.0	25.4%
Retail	6.6	14.9%	7.0	14.3%
Hotels	2.7	35.4%	2.8	35.4%
Sub-total of job creating schemes	4.5	21.7%	5.0	20.0%
Housing	5.2	21.6%	6.8	14.6%
Total	4.6	21.7%	5.1	19.6%

Note:

The percentage figures express the relationship between the net amount of public expenditure in a project to that invested by the private sector. If a project has a 1:1 gearing ratio then the percentage that private sector investment represents in relation to the public sector contribution will be 100%.

provide their own estimates of its market value and calculated the gearing on that basis.

326 In order to ascertain actual private investment we also asked each developer to state the actual level of costs incurred in the project. We found that the majority of developers rarely undertook a detailed review of costs incurred on completion.

327 Where developers have failed to provide any data to assist in assessing actual private sector investment we have had to assume that the projected costs and values were actually incurred and achieved.

328 Tables 6.2 and 6.2b show the actual and projected gearing ratios for each project as well as the average for each development use type. We have also attempted to demonstrate the relationship of projected and actual grant to the total cost of a scheme.

329 Table 6.3 below summarises the performance of projects by use type group in terms of whether the level of private sector inputs levered by the grant regime improved, worsened or remained the same over the duration of the project.

330 In 33 out of the 36 projects sampled the gearing ratio either stayed the same or improved. This was as a result of the project being sold or valued at a level that either corresponded or exceeded that contained in the original grant application. Of the 3 projects which witnessed a worsening in gearing ratio 2 involved projects where values had declined although investment made on the site had remained either constant or increased above that contained in the application. Only one project, therefore, involved a situation where grant brought forward output which both cost less and was worth less than that projected.

SCHEME OUTPUTS

331 All grant aided schemes must provide jobs or private sector housing (City Grant Guidance notes). There are therefore two areas of 'relevant outputs'.

- Job creation
- Dwellings completed

Job Creation

332 Estimates of the number of permanent jobs were obtained from the occupier survey. The gross number of jobs was adjusted to take into account displacement; the methodology for ex post evaluation we adopted is explained in paragraphs 159–172 above. Paragraphs 190–194 went on to cover the appraisers' methodology for ex ante appraisals explaining that they took a simplified approach to estimating displacement and compensated by "aiming off" to a low cost per job target.

333 By dividing the net grant awarded by jobs housed we assessed the gross cost per job. We then divided the net grant awarded by the net additional jobs to determine the net cost per job.

334 This exercise was carried out to calculate both the cost per job housed in a project and the cost per net additional job. In addition, all schemes created temporary jobs during construction. These are not included in our calculation of scheme output, for reasons explained in Chapter 3.

335 Tables 6.4 and 6.4b overleaf shows the projected and actual jobs, (both gross and net) housed for each scheme and type of scheme.

336 An interesting pattern emerges in terms of the variance between projected and actual jobs in a scheme. It is apparent that the majority of schemes (19 out of 31 that created jobs) involved an over optimistic assessment of job creation for the reasons set out in para 332.. This was particularly apparent in the retail and office sectors.

337 Table 6.5 demonstrates this on a use type basis.

338 The Hotel sector (despite a small sample size) appears to perform well although Paradise Circus was both an hotel and office project assisted by

Table 6.3 – Gearing Performance			
Use Type	Improved	Stayed the same	Worsened
Offices	7 (70%)	2 (20%)	1 (10%)
Industrial	5 (45%)	5 (45%)	1 (9%)
Retail	2 (33%)	3 (50%)	1 (17%)
Hotels	1 (33%)	2 (66%)	–
Housing	4 (66%)	2 (34%)	–
All	19 (53%)	14 (39%)	3 (8%)

Table 6.4 – Projected and actual job creation			
	Projected	Actual housed (Gross)	Actual net additional
OFFICES			
Birmingham, 3–5 St Paul's Square	30	10	10
Birmingham, Snowhill Station	80	472	0
Leicester, Arnhem House	210	279	172
Manchester, Albion House	60	9	0
Newcastle, 43/49 Grey Street	135	27	0
Nottingham, Newcastle House	258	250	80
Nottingham, Stoney Street	125	200	4
Oldham, Union Street	190	46	20
Sheffield, Huttons	82	75	22
Southwark, Archbishop Temple Business Units	150	122	114
INDUSTRIAL			
Birmingham, Garrison Lane	200	80	37
Birmingham, IMI Holdford Park	1,000	894	418
Birmingham, Newhall Hill	50	95	0
Birmingham, Startpoint Industrial Units	136	90	19
Boldon Business Park	300	199	183
Hartlepool, Hartlepool Business Park	300	29	0
Nottingham, Beechdale Engineering	195	220	220
Nottingham, Southglade Park	100	92	3
Oldham, MCM Ltd	16	25	0
Oldham, Stamford Mill	100	161	128
Southwark, Priter Way Arches	141	4	4
RETAIL			
Birmingham, One Stop, Perry Bar	1,000	516	282
Bolton, Bark Street	675	389	382
Gateshead, Felling Town Centre	100	81	59
Hull, Bransholme North	61	66	33
Middlesbrough, Zetland Road (also included office development)	147	125	45
South Shields, Catherine Street	20	26	8
HOTELS			
Birmingham, Paradise Circus (also included office development)	100	257	180
Manchester, Midland Hotel	210	343	343
Nottingham, Rutland Square Hotel	100	89	89

Table 6.4B – Projected and actual job creation by use type			
Offices	1,320	1,490	422
Industrial	2,538	1,889	1,012
Retail	2,003	1,203	809
Hotels	410	689	612
Total	6,271	5,271	2,855

Note: Projected Jobs – projected at the time of the grant application using the "aim off" technique described in para 322
Actual Jobs Housed – total full time equivalent jobs in project
Actual Net Additional Jobs – after full allowance for displacement

Table 6.5 – Projected and actual job creation by sector				
Use Type	Jobs Housed (Gross)		Jobs Housed (Net)	
	Improvement on Projected	Decline on Projected	Improvement on Projected	Decline on Projected
Offices	3 (30%)	7 (70%)	0 (0%)	10 (100%)
Industrial	4 (36%)	7 (64%)	2 (18%)	9 (82%)
Retail	1 (17%)	5 (83%)	0 (0%)	6 (100%)
Hotels	2 (67%)	1 (33%)	2 (67%)	1 (33%)
Housing (Hull, Coltman Street)	0 (%)	1 (%)	0 (%)	1 (100%)
All	10 (32%)	21 (68%)	4 (10%)	27 (90%)

UDG and employment projections were undertaken quite crudely. The Midland Hotel, Manchester has also performed well in terms of job creation.

339 When actual net additional job creation was compared with that projected only 4 out of 31 schemes recorded an improvement in output performance. These included the hotel projects described above and two industrial projects (Beechdale Engineering, Nottingham and Stamford Mill, Oldham).

340 Tables 6.6 and 6.6b below demonstrate performance in relation to cost per gross job across each use type sector. In order to compare projects in terms of cost per unit output we applied RPI indices to bring all net grant awards to a base value.

- Base date adopted August 1991.
- Nominal – actual prices: costs incurred at date of application.
- August 1991 prices: grant award inflated using RPI in order to aid comparison across sample over 8 year period.
- Date of grant award ie the date when DoE "bought" the benefits/outputs of the programme.

341 Table 6.7 and 6.7b shows the actual cost per net job after allowing for displacement attributable to occupiers stating that there were either suitable alternative premises in the area or that they merely transferred their operation from elsewhere in the Inner Area.

342 In 24 out of 31 cases the project created net additional jobs. Only seven were deemed to have yielded 'no output'. These were:

- Snowhill Station, Birmingham
- Albion House, Manchester
- 43, 49 Grey Street, Newcastle
- Newhall Hill, Birmingham
- Business Park, Hartlepool
- MCM Ltd, Oldham
- Courtauld's Warehouse (primarily a housing project), Hull.

343 Projects that recorded 'no output' were either office or industrial schemes. These two sectors also recorded a high level of variance in the actual outturn cost per net additional job. For example six out of the 21 projects in this group recorded a net cost per job of below £10,000 whilst four projects had costs in excess of £100,000 per job (excluding those with no output).

Table 6.6 – Projected and actual costs per job housed in the project				
	Projected cost per job		Actual cost per job housed	
	Nominal (£)	1991 Prices (£)	Nominal (£)	1991 Prices (£)
OFFICES				
Birmingham, 3–5 St Paul's Square	3,400	5,527	10,200	16,580
Birmingham, Snowhill Station	2,500	3,862	381	589
Leicester, Arnhem House	3,372	4,027	2,537	3,030
Manchester, Albion House	5,017	6,241	33,444	41,604
Newcastle, 43/49 Grey Street	3,611	4,363	10,376	12,535
Nottingham, Newcastle House	2,849	3,753	1,996	2,629
Nottingham, Stoney Street (primarily a car park)	7,520	10,238	4,700	6,399
Oldham, Union Street	3,389	5,124	14,000	21,166
Sheffield, Huttons	3,290	3,928	3,182	3,800
Southwark, Archbishop Temple Business Units	3,333	3,880	4,098	4,771
INDUSTRIAL				
Birmingham, Garrison Lane	2,850	3,418	7,125	8,546
Birmingham, IMI Holdford Park	5,685	8,896	4,582	7,169
Birmingham, Newhall Hill	1,400	2,153	737	1,133
Birmingham, Startpoint Industrial Units	2,081	2,496	3,144	3,772
Boldon Business Park	4,103	4,768	6,186	7,188
Hartlepool, Hartlepool Business Park	2,115	2,458	21,883	25,429
Nottingham, Beechdale Engineering	5,410	7,127	4,795	6,317
Nottingham, Southglade Park	3,634	4,844	3,880	5,173
Oldham, MCM Ltd	1,938	2,598	1,240	1,663
Oldham, Stamford Mill	2,247	3,382	1,396	2,101
Southwark, Priter Way Arches	3,723	4,312	119,363	138,226
RETAIL				
Birmingham, One Stop, Perry Bar	2,620	3,321	5,078	6,436
Bolton, Bark Street	6,667	9,634	10,887	15,732
Gateshead, Felling Town Centre	5,750	7,982	7,099	9,854
Hull, Bransholme North	5,410	7,588	4,204	5,897
Middlesbrough, Zetland Road (also included office development)	4,497	5,792	5,288	6,812
South Shields, Catherine Street	3,700	5,234	2,846	4,026

continued

Table 6.6 continued – Projected and actual costs per job housed in the project				
	Projected cost per job		Actual cost per job housed	
	Nominal (£)	1991 Prices (£)	Nominal (£)	1991 Prices (£)
HOTELS				
Birmingham, Paradise Circus (also included office development)	46,806	68,974	18,212	26,838
Manchester, Midland Hotel	10,476	14,604	6,414	8,941
Nottingham, Rutland Square Hotel	7,380	9,354	8,292	10,510

Table 6.6B – Projected and actual costs per job housed in the project by use type				
Offices	3,703	4,856	2,948	3,879
Industrial	4,205	5,932	4,780	6,621
Retail	4,373	6,011	7,018	9,629
Hotels	18,582	26,584	11,057	15,819
Total	5,093	7,081	5,593	7,735

Note: Projected Jobs – projected at the time of the grant application using the "aim off" technique described in para 322
 Actual Jobs Housed – total full time equivalent jobs in project
 Actual Net Additional Jobs – after full allowance for displacement

Table 6.7 – Projected and actual costs per net job				
	Projected cost per job		Actual cost per net job	
	Nominal (£)	Real (£)	Nominal (£)	Real (£)
OFFICES				
Birmingham, 3–5 St Paul's Square	3,400	5,527	10,200	16,580
Birmingham, Snowhill Station	2,500	3,862	No output	
Leicester, Arnhem House	3,372	4,027	4,116	4,915
Manchester, Albion House	5,017	6,241	No output	
Newcastle, 43/49 Grey Street	3,611	4,363	No output	
Nottingham, Newcastle House	2,849	3,753	6,237	8,216
Nottingham, Stoney Street (primarily a car park dev)	7,520	10,238	235,000	319,934
Oldham, Union Street	3,389	5,124	32,000	48,681
Sheffield, Huttons	3,290	3,928	10,848	12,953
Southwark, Archbishop Temple Business Units	3,333	3,880	4,386	5,106
INDUSTRIAL				
Birmingham, Garrison Lane	2,850	3,418	15,405	18,478

continued

Table 6.7 continued – Projected and actual costs per net job				
	Projected cost per job		Actual cost per net job	
	Nominal (£)	Real (£)	Nominal (£)	Real (£)
Birmingham, IMI Holdford Park	5,685	8,896	9,799	15,333
Birmingham, Newhall Hill	1,400	2,153	No output	
Birmingham, Startpoint Industrial Units	2,081	2,496	14,895	17,866
Boldon Business Park	4,103	4,768	6,726	7,816
Hartlepool, Hartlepool Business Park	2,115	2,458	No output	
Nottingham, Beechdale Engineering	5,410	7,127	4,795	6,317
Nottingham, Southglade Park	3,634	4,844	119,000	158,627
Oldham, MCM Ltd	1,938	2,598	No output	
Oldham, Stamford Mill	2,247	3,382	1,756	2,627
Southwark, Priter Way Arches	3,723	4,312	119,363	138,226
RETAIL				
Birmingham, One Stop, Perry Bar	2,620	3,321	9,291	11,776
Bolton, Bark Street	6,667	9,634	11,086	16,020
Gateshead, Felling Town Centre	5,750	7,982	9,746	13,529
Hull, Bransholme North	5,410	7,588	8,408	11,794
Middlesbrough, Zetland Road (also included office development)	4,497	5,792	14,689	18,992
South Shields, Catherine Street	3,700	5,234	9,250	13,085
HOTELS				
Birmingham, Paradise Circus (also included office development)	46,806	68,974	26,003	38,319
Manchester, Midland Hotel	10,476	14,604	6,414	8,941
Nottingham, Rutland Square Hotel	7,380	9,354	8,292	10,510

Table 6.7B – Projected and actual costs per net job by use type				
Offices	3,703	4,856	10,409	13,696
Industrial	4,205	5,932	8,923	12,358
Retail	4,373	6,011	10,436	14,319
Hotels	18,582	26,584	12,449	17,810
Total	5,093	7,081	10,327	14,280

Note: Projected Jobs – projected at the time of the grant application using the "aim off" technique described in para 322

Actual Cost Per Jobs – after full allowance for displacement

344 By contrast retail projects all recorded net job creation, and the cost levels recorded were all between £11,776 (One Stop Perry Bar, Birmingham) and £18,992 (Zetland Road, Middlesbrough).

345 Finally the hotel sector, despite only having a sample size of three projects performed well. With the exception of Paradise Circus, Birmingham the net cost per job of the two remaining projects was low.

346 When all the figures are analysed on a use type basis the range between the sectors is surprisingly low (Industrial £12,538 per net additional job to hotels £17,810 per net additional job).

Dwellings Completed

347 In five out of six housing projects the developer completed the scheme as described in the grant application. Only in the case of the project in (Southglade Park, Nottingham) did the developer fail to complete the project. (See table 6.8 below).

Table 6.9 shows the pattern that emerges when the cost per unit of output is calculated.

348 Despite the sale by the developer of Southglade Park, Nottingham none of the projects reported a worsening in cost per unit output and in only one case (Coltman Street, Hull) did cost per unit output remain the same.

349 In five out of six cases there was a reduction in public sector cost per unit output reflecting the buoyancy of the housing market in the mid-late 1980s. We did not, however investigate any housing schemes in the 'post-boom' era and suggest this picture would be significantly different had we had a sample including projects developed later in the market cycle.

Table 6.8 – Projected and actual completion of dwellings		
	Projected	Actual
Birmingham, The Parade	72	72
Hull, Coltman Street	101	101
Hull, Courtauld's Warehouse	27	27
Nottingham, Southglade Park	200	100
Nottingham, Mundella Court	74	74
Oldham, Bank Top Mill	120	120
TOTAL	594	494

Table 6.9 – Projected and actual costs per completed dwelling				
	Projected Cost per dwelling		Actual cost per dwelling	
	Nominal £	Real £	Nominal £	Real £
Birmingham, The Parade	7,542	10,341	7,376	10,114
Hull, Coltman Street	9,426	13,250	9,426	13,250
Hull, Courtauld's Warehouse	9,037	12,676	8,481	11,897
Nottingham, Southglade Park	2,683	3,577	1,891	2,521
Nottingham, Mundella Court	2,924	3,811	0	0
Oldham, Bank Top Mill	3,255	4,094	417	524
All	4,853	6,589	3,950	5,471

A COMPARISON OF UDG, URG AND CITY GRANT

Introduction

350 Our evaluation has covered grant aided projects from 1983 to the present date and therefore encompasses UDG, URG and City Grant schemes.

351 UDG operated in the period between 1983 and 1988, with URG being added in the latter part of this period in order to promote area regeneration. In practice few URGs were awarded. They were administered in a manner consistent with UDG practice but, like City Grant for which they were the pilot, the requirement that 25% of the grant cost should be met by the local authority was dropped. City Grant then replaced both UDG and URG in May 1988. The basis of all three grants is similar in that they all provided gap funding for projects where it was considered that they would not be able to go ahead unaided because of inner city factors and which offered value for money in terms of relevant inner city outputs.

352 In our sample 36 projects were evaluated and these have been classified under the use-type headings of offices, industrial, retail, hotels and housing. The spread between each grant regime was as follows:

	UDG	URG	CG	TOTAL
Offices	5	1	4	10
Industrial	7	–	4	11
Retail	5	–	1	6
Hotels	2	–	1	3
Housing	6	–	–	6
All	25	1	10	36

353 In comparing the grants it is important to realise that the outputs yielded from completed projects vary over the development cycle and that comparison of VFM across grant and use types should involve careful consideration of the volatile nature of market conditions over the period.

354 A comparison of performance measures is shown below. In general it is difficult to draw conclusions on URG performance as it was in operation for a relatively short time and was also supplemental to UDG. It is however possible to compare UDG with City Grant on gearing and cost per job as shown below. While this analysis does highlight differences in output levels this is more likely to be a factor of the timing of projects rather than a difference in approach. Both schemes provide gap funding for property related projects and their objectives and aims were in general consistent.

Gearing Projected (Actual in Brackets)

	UDG	URG	CG	ALL GRANTS
Offices	5.1 (5.8)	3.9 (7.5)	7.6 (8.1)	6.0 (6.8)
Industrial	3.2 (4.1)	No sample	3.7 (3.9)	3.3 (4.1)
Retail	6.3 (6.9)	No sample	7.3 (7.3)	6.6 (7.0)
Hotels	2.4 (2.4)	No sample	5.3 (6.8)	2.7 (2.8)
Housing	5.2 (6.8)	No sample	None	5.2 (6.8)
All	4.1 (4.7)	3.9 (7.5)	6.0 (6.2)	4.6 (5.1)

Cost per job (August 1991 prices in brackets)

	UDG	URG	CG	ALL GRANTS
Offices	20,744 (29,424)	No output	5,606 (6,658)	10,409 (13,696)
Industrial	7,945 (11,720)	No sample	12,748 (14,855)	8,923 (12,358)
Retail	11,048 (15,680)	No sample	9,291 (11,776)	10,436 (14,319)
Hotels	13,156 (19,052)	No sample	8,292 (10,510)	12,449 (17,810)
All	10,899 (15,750)	No output	8,713 (10,584)	10,327 (14,280)

CONCLUSIONS

355 Despite a lack of reliable data from developers, in particular relating to costs incurred, we estimate that the targets set for levering private capital i.e. gearing were almost completely achieved or exceeded. Only at Priter Way Arches, Southwark did the award of grant result in the bringing forward of a development which both cost less to build and was valued lower than that projected at appraisal stage.

356 The data regarding ex post measures of value for money has to be interpreted with extreme caution and appreciation of what it represents. Value for money is calculated by ascertaining the net grant awarded to a developer after deducting clawback. The clawback depends on the relationship between costs and realised value. It is, by its nature, extremely sensitive to market conditions prevailing at the time the development is sold. VFM as an ex post indicator is therefore distorted by the nature of market value movements (and therefore grant net of clawback) over time. This makes comparisons between schemes difficult and limits the usefulness of ex post VFM measures for drawing policy conclusions.

357 Mundella Court, Nottingham, is a good example where the actual sales value realised by the developer had, by the end of the development, risen to twice the original amount included in the grant application. As a result the grant was totally 'clawed back' giving a zero cost per dwelling. In contrast Courtaulds Warehouse and Coltman Street in Hull show relatively low VFM as they were completed prior to the onset of the "housing boom" which emerged between the first quarter of 1988 and the third quarter of 1989, and resulted in prices in the area rising by 50%. Had these schemes been developed a year or so later then clawback would have been substantially higher and VFM would have improved accordingly. The effect of timing therefore distorts analysis of VFM and its implications for ex post programme assessment.

7 Policy conclusions and recommendations

INTRODUCTION

358 At the beginning of this report we outlined our objectives as being:

- to evaluate the success of the sampled grant aided projects in meeting their objectives;
- to evaluate the success of these projects in contributing to the wider regeneration of the local area;
- to identify success factors associated with the achievement (or otherwise) of the objectives;
- to make recommendations for future policy formulation.

359 We have addressed the first three of these objectives in our previous chapters. The purpose of this chapter is to bring all our conclusions into one section, in order to address the fourth.

POLICY CONCLUSIONS

360 Here we are concerned with two components of policy, these being:

- objectives;
- policy tools.

Policy objectives

361 The aims of City Grant and its predecessors are to encourage major private sector capital schemes which would otherwise be unable to proceed because, as a result of their inner city sites and locations, costs exceed values. The grant regime is demand led.

362 Initially the UDG guidance notes outlined a set of objectives including ones:

"to promote the economic and physical regeneration of inner urban areas by levering private sector investment into such areas"

and

"to make a demonstrable contribution to meeting the special social needs of inner urban areas and

creating a climate of confidence for the private sector".

The City Grant guidance notes (2nd edition) state that:

"City Grant is provided to support private sector capital projects which benefit rundown inner city areas and which, because of their inner city site or location, cannot proceed without assistance".

363 Advice is also given on value for money (cost per job and cost per dwelling) and gearing. Although the averages for UDG are presented, the Department has always made it clear that these are not intended as targets.

364 We appreciate that City Grant and its predecessors have aimed to be flexible – to allow applicants to bring forward whatever projects seem to them to make most commercial sense. This has led the Department to issue Guidance Notes, first for UDG and then for City Grant, which, while clear on the general objectives and broad criteria, avoid presenting applicants with rigid rules or targets. Similarly the appraisers, especially in the earlier years, were given a broad steer but left to approach each application on its merits. This procedure may have been safeguarded by secondary appraisal and referral of cases to Ministers for decision but it has complicated our task in trying to find standard measures for evaluating the successes and failures of such a wide range of projects.

365 It would have assisted evaluation if the Guidance Notes had included more explicit performance targets for projects, and if appraisers' case papers had given a fuller account of the direct and indirect benefits each project was expected to produce. But we note that case papers produced in the last two or three years – and which therefore fall outside our sample – follow a more standard format which addresses these and other issues much more clearly. This should make it that much easier to establish whether, when these later projects have been completed, they achieve their intended outputs. Moreover, we do not think that this question is confined simply to post hoc evaluation. It costs applicants a great deal to put applications together. We remain of the opinion that any future Guidance Notes should give a fuller explanation of targets

partly to help with evaluation, but also so that applicants can more easily judge their chances of success before incurring expense. These targets could include for example a better description of the environmental and social objectives because it is evident from our sample that some private sector applicants were not clear what weight might be given to these.

366 A further observation is that the economic objectives of the policy, presently considered in terms of capital investment, job creation and numbers of housing units might be, in the Guidance Notes at least expressed more widely, to counteract any bias towards low cost, high floorspace buildings – wider measures could include:

- output generation;
- income and wealth creation;
- local trading links.

367 While the analysis of additional economic benefits would improve the targeting of the policy, we accept that this benefit would have to be weighed against the additional work that would be required at the appraisal stage and the danger of removing the simplicity of the grant process which the private sector now understands and which is one of its great strengths.

Policy tools

368 City Grant is a gap funding property development tool, which relies on the private sector identifying an opportunity, bringing that opportunity to the public sector, and negotiating the minimum level of assistance required to realise the aims of the policy.

369 This mechanism has the following advantages:

- it is straightforward to operate and is now understood by the development market,
- it is private sector demand driven and only sites and buildings where the private sector perceive that there is a market potential are considered. This maximises the efficiency of the allocation of public sector resources,
- it is inexpensive to operate,
- the private sector bears any abortive costs of projects,
- it is open and transparent. The scope for abuse at any level is very limited,
- it has been successful across a wide range and size of schemes, regardless of location,
- it has initiated true public/private sector collaboration,
- cost per job figures compare favourably with other forms of public sector job creation mechanisms,
- cost per dwelling figures compare favourably with other forms of public housing support,

- take up has been good, despite a depressed market in recent years.

370 However the policy tool is not without its weaknesses. In particular:

- Spatial targeting has changed only marginally since the introduction of UDG over ten years ago and there has been no change since the 57 UP areas were selected in 1986.
- The demand led nature of the grant produces a very uneven distribution of investment. Some of the 57 areas have, for no obvious reasons, secured far more grant than others.
- Within each of the 57 authority areas the grants have been attracted to sites offering the best development opportunities, rather than to areas of more acute need.
- Grants have tended to favour larger projects offering low cost commercial and industrial floorspace or low cost housing rather than smaller scale more imaginative projects.
- It does not address the basic causes of poor regional or local growth. In areas of clear and sustained market failure, theoretical best practise (Lord Kaldor) suggests that this growth comes from relative improvements in the performance of the local trading base (reducing imports and/or increasing exports.) Job creation (although linked to this) is in fact a secondary or consequent factor in the creation of economic growth.

371 Looking at the sample as a whole, many projects did not achieve the cost per job targets set in the case papers or the averages for approved projects set out in the 1988 edition of the City Grant Guidance Notes, the version current at that time. Our own analysis shows that far fewer net additional jobs were achieved. But it also shows that, because grant decisions were based on an awareness of the likely underestimate of displacement losses, and were therefore "aimed off" at a low cost per job criterion, the actual cost per net additional job was reasonable in relation to quoted averages from other job creating policies. In any case cost per job is only part of the story, the projects also produced environmental, social and other benefits appropriate to City Grant's role as an urban renewal policy. A more explicitly economic policy would however have to consider both the root causes of local economic growth and the use of industrial policy tools to meet its objectives.

The next section discusses the policy implications of these findings.

POLICY RECOMMENDATIONS

Objectives

372 We recommend consideration as to whether:

- the range of objectives is wide enough
- objectives are sufficiently well specified

Each of these will be briefly discussed in turn.

373 A wider range of economic objectives would be helpful if the full spectrum of influences which contribute towards the creation of economic growth are to be covered adequately. We have made some suggestions at Appendix 2.

374 Although social and environment benefits may have been considered by the Appraisers, this was not always apparent from the sample case paper. The Department could be more explicit about its objectives. From our analysis City Grant generates significant environmental benefits and also produces social and community benefits. While more explicit reference and quantification has been included in successive Guidance Notes, greater account of these benefits could be ensured by using techniques similar to those adopted in our study.

375 As previously remarked, we have found it unnecessarily difficult in some cases to measure the effectiveness of projects in meeting their objectives because the targets were not specified with sufficient clarity in the case papers. More recent cases show that this problem has been recognised but more definite targets on issues such as job creation, gearing and cost per job would go some way towards overcoming this problem and would make the evaluation process much more precise. It may be appropriate to attach a policy effectiveness target to each objective.

376 The Department has always shied away from publishing this kind of target, in the belief that it will inhibit applicants and choke off "good schemes". Looking at the samples in our study however, we think that the schemes would still have come forward, even if it were known that the Department were working to certain published targets.

377 Arguments against publishing targets might be reduced if the Department made it absolutely clear that they were looking for a "score" across the whole matrix of targets, not against any one. For appraisal purposes, a scoring system could be devised. We see no reason why applicants would be intimidated by this. Indeed, we think it would be seen as helpful, and would reduce work weeding out good and bad cases presently undertaken in Regional offices.

Alternative policy tools

378 We know that the Government is considering new ways of delivering assistance to deprived areas, and it is clear from the recently published discussion paper on the Urban Regeneration Agency (URA) that the URA is to be constituted in such a way as to address some of the points we have made.

379 Price Waterhouse has made a considered response to the URA consultation paper, but as far as City Grant is concerned, we believe it important not to throw out the baby with the bathwater. The appraisal system behind City Grant has been extremely successful as a delivery mechanism. Its advantages are quite capable of being preserved when/if delivery becomes the responsibility of the URA.

IN CONCLUSION

380 Whilst we recognise that City Grant is being considered for incorporation within a comprehensive grant regime which incorporates Derelict Land Grant, we believe that the ideas which we have developed during our analysis of the regime have relevance to future urban regeneration policies and programmes which are currently under consideration.

381 City Grant itself has been a useful initiative in terms both of its effectiveness and its contribution to the rapidly evolving debate on the future of urban policy. The Department has assembled a considerable fund of experience in administering it. We feel it is important to appreciate that our criticisms are of minor importance in relation to the scale of investment and economic development which has been achieved since 1983.

APPENDIX 1 : OCCUPIER QUESTIONAIRE

APPENDIX 1 : OCCUPIER QUESTIONNAIRE

DEPARTMENT OF ENVIRONMENT

CITY GRANT EVALUATION

NAME:	
POSITION:	
COMPANY:	
ADDRESS: POSTCODE:	
TELEPHONE NO:	
DATE:	
BUSINESS UNDERTAKEN AT THIS ADDRESS:	

	SECTION A - PREMISES		
		Month	Year
Q1	When did you first occupy these premises?		
		YES	
Q2	Were you the first occupier of the premises. (Please tick box) If Yes - Go to Q4.	NO	
Q3	Do you have the name and current address of the previous occupier? Name: _____ Address:_____ _____ _____ _____	NO	
Q4	Was your business previously at another address? Street _____ Town _____ Post Code _____	YES	
		NO	
Q5	How large were your previous premises?		^{2}ft
Q6	Have you vacated these previous premises?	YES	
		NO	

SECTION B - PREMISES SELECTION

Q7	Why did you move to your existing premises? Did you require: (Tick all relevant boxes and circle <u>most</u> important reason)		
		1.	Larger premises
		2.	Smaller premises
		3.	Additional premises
		4.	Better location
		5.	Higher Quality
		6.	Labour Availability
		7.	To Retain key staff
		8.	Other (specify below)

Q7 Why did you move to your existing premises? Did you require:
(Tick all relevant boxes and circle <u>most</u> important reason)

1.	Larger premises	1
2.	Smaller premises	2
3.	Additional premises	3
4.	Better location	4
5.	Higher Quality	5
6.	Labour Availability	6
7.	To Retain key staff	7
8.	Other (specify below)	8

_____
_____
_____
_____
_____
_____
_____

| Q8 | Were alternative premises considered? (If NO - Go to Q11) | YES | |
| | | NO | |

Q9	Where were these (next best alternative)?	
	Address _____	
	_____	
	_____ Post Code ____	
	_____	

| Q10 | Were these premises less than 10 years old? | YES | |
| | | NO | |

| Q11 | Had they been previously occupied? | YES | |
| | | NO | |

68

SECTION B - PREMISES SELECTION Cont'd	

Q12	Did you prefer your existing premises over the next best alternative because they offered:-

(Tick all relevant boxes and circle most important reason)

1	Lower price		1
2	Higher quality		2
3	Better lease terms		3
4	Better location		4
5	Better environment		5
6	Immediate availability		6
7	Other (specify below)		7

_____

_____

_____

_____

_____

Q13	If your existing premises had not been available would you have:

(tick one box only)

1.	Stayed in previous premises	1
2.	Occupied other premises within area	2
3.	Occupied other premises outside area	3
4.	Ceased trading	4
5.	Not opened (new business)	5
6.	Other (specify below)	6

_____

_____

_____

_____

_____

(See attached map with identified area boundary)

Q14	Did you know the premises had received Government grant assistance? (If NO – Go to Q14)	YES	
		NO	
Q15	Did this affect your decision?	YES	
		NO	

	SECTION C - EMPLOYMENT		
Q16	How many people (1) are permanently employed at this address? Full time (*less than 24 hrs p/week) *Part time	persons	
		persons	
Q17	How many people were permanently employed when you first occupied the premises? Full time *Part time	persons	
		persons	
Q18	How many people were employed at your **previous premises**? Full time *Part time	persons	
		persons	
Q19	How many people are still employed by you at your **previous premises**? Full time *Part time	persons	
		persons	
Q20	Of the employees at this address what percentage are:-		
	1. Manual	1	%
	2. Clerical/Administrative	2	%
	3. Technical	3	%
	4. Managerial/Professional	4	%
			100 %

(1) All references in this section are to permanently employed staff.

SECTION C - EMPLOYMENT Cont'd				
Q21	How many people do you expect to employee at this address in one years time? (*less than 24 hrs p/week)	Full time *Part time		persons persons
Q22	Approximately what percentage of your employees **at this address** live within the area outlined on the attached map?	Full time *Part time	<25% 25-49% 50-75% >75%	
Q23	Approximately what proportion of your employees **at your previous address** lived (or live) within the same area?	Full time *Part time	<25% 25-49% 50-75% >75%	
Q24	When a new vacancy arises will you seek to employ somebody from within this area? (If YES - Go to Q24)		YES NO	
Q25	Why would you not seek to employ somebody from within this area? (Tick all relevant boxes and circle most **important**) 1. Skill Shortage 2. Pay levels too high 3. Too few candidates 4. Other (specify below) _____ _____ _____ _____ _____		1 2 3 4	

SECTION D - YOUR MARKET

Q26	In which business sector does your company operate?	
	1. Manufacturing	1
	2. Warehousing & Distribution	2
	3. Professional & Business Services	3
	4. Retailing	4
	5. Leisure & Hotel	5
	6. Other (specify below)	6

_____

_____

_____

_____

_____

Q27	What proportion of demand for your goods and services has been:-	
	1. Transferred from previous premises	%
	2. New Business generated since occupation	%
	3. Won from Competition since occupation	%
		100%

Q28	What proportion of your customers are located:-	
	1. Within the area on the map	%
	2. Within your Region(2)	%
	3. Within Rest of UK	%
	4. Overseas	%
		100%

(2) ....

72

	SECTION D - YOUR MARKET Cont'd	
Q29	What proportion of your competitors are located:-	
	1. Within the area on the map	%
	2. Within your Region(2)	%
	3. Within the rest of the UK	%
	4. Overseas	%
		100%
Q30	What proportion of your suppliers are located:-	
	1. Within the area on the map	%
	2. Within your Region(2)	%
	3. Within the rest of the UK	%
	4. Overseas	%
		100%
Q31	Was proximity to customers complete or supplies most important in choosing your existing location:	
	Customers	
	Competition	
	Suppliers	
	None of the above	
Q32	What was your turnover at this site in the last financial year?	£
Q33	What was the capital investment in your business following your move to these premises (ignoring any costs for **acquiring** the premises)?	£
Q34	How much of this investment would have been made if you had not moved to these premises?	£

(2) ....

Thank you for your assistance in completing this questionnaire. If there are any other issues or comments you wish to raise please do so in the space provided overleaf.

Appendix 2

OTHER INDICATORS OF ECONOMIC IMPACT

In this appendix indicators of economic impact which are not included in the DOE/Treasury approach yet which we consider shed light on a wider range of economic effects are described.

Other indicators of displacement

Employment Displacement will occur where, ceteris paribus, a firm housed in an assisted scheme wins market share from their competitors (as a result of their move to new premises); it is of relevance to this review where those competitors are in the inner area. Respondents to questionnaires provided information on the sources of the business conducted in assisted schemes. Responses are categorised by business type in Table A2.1 below. The figures relate only to respondents and refer to all competitors – not just those in the inner area. It should be stressed that these figures are not presented as estimates of employment displacement, but as an indication of the source of business carried out in the assisted premises. As such they may indicate the propensity of these business categories to displace employment in the inner area.

Thus, for the sample as a whole, almost half of all business was transferred to the assisted premises from the premises previously occupied by the business. Occupiers identified only a relatively small proportion of their business as being won from competitors after their move. However these figures do need to be treated with a degree of caution, as the distinction in the respondent's mind between new business and that won from competitors may be blurred. Particularly in the retail sector it is difficult for a branch manager to distinguish between a new customer and one who previously shopped at another stor This may, in part, explain the relatively high level of new business identified by occupiers in retail schemes. A similar argument can be applied to the hotel schemes in the sample. It is possible that more reliable figures have been supplied by industrial and office occupiers where markets

Table A2.1 – Source of Business (%)					
Sample	Office	Industrial	Retail	Hotel	
Transferred from previous premises	54	66	21	25	49
New business generated since transfer	39	29	63	46	40
New business won from competitors after transfer	7	6	18	29	11
TOTAL	100	101	102	100	100

Table A2.2 – Location of Competitors (%)					
Location	Office	Industrial	Retail	Hotel	Sample
Inner Area	49	17	71	50	44
Region	19	29	23	46	27
Rest of UK	25	49	6	4	26
Overseas	7	5	0	0	3
TOTAL	100	100	100	100	100

Table A2.3 – Location of Customers (%)					
Location	Office	Industrial	Retail	Hotel	Sample
Inner Area	31	17	71	14	34
Region	39	33	25	41	34
Rest of UK	22	45	4	37	28
Overseas	8	5	0	8	4
TOTAL	100	100	100	100	100

are more clearly defined and customer/supplier relationships may last over a series of transactions.

Respondents were also asked to supply information on the location of their main competitors in an effort to further investigate the propensity of each business category to displace employment in the inner area. Again, these figures are not proxies for employment displacement but give an indication of the levels of competition within the inner area.

The high proportion of competitors for retail occupiers within the inner area suggests a strong propensity for displacement of retail employment at the inner area level, on the assumption that the total volume of retail activity in the inner area does not increase to accommodate the new occupiers. Both office and hotel occupiers have identified half of their competitors as being located in the inner area and again the propensity for displacement is substantial if the market does not expand to meet the new capacity. Industrial scheme occupiers identify the majority of their competitors as existing at the supra regional level with displacement potential at the UK level.

Information on the location of customers can be used as a cross check on competitor location in a further attempt to quantify the potential for inner area displacement. A customer base in the inner area, in conjunction with a large proportion of inner area based competitors, suggests employment displacement may occur in the inner area. Table A2.3 summarises the information we collected on customer origins.

Perhaps not surprisingly retail occupiers identify a large number of their customers originating in the inner area. However there are dangers in adopting these findings as representative of retail schemes in general. Whilst competitors and customers may be concentrated in the inner area on completion of the development this may not have been the case previously. To take a specific example, Bolton shopping centre may have attracted inner area customers back to the town centre when previously they may have shopped in Manchester or Bury. Individual shop managers when responding to the questionnaire may well identify their competitors as located within Bolton and indeed within the Centre. However at the aggregate level the competition for the Centre (ie alternative comparison

shopping facilities) may be at the regional level (eg Manchester). As a result employment displacement may not occur at the inner area level (which is the level of relevance to this study) but may well occur at the regional level.

Whilst office occupiers identified the largest proportion of their competitors at the inner area the greatest proportion of customers is at the regional level. This is to be expected as a function of land economics with inner areas of towns and cities providing agglomeration economies (primarily in the areas of transportation and labour) to office occupiers wishing to service regional markets. This concentration of customers at the Regional level will tend to offset employment displacement at the inner area level.

Industrial occupiers identify the largest proportions of both their customers and competitors as being located at the supra regional level. The propensity for employment displacement is therefore relatively low for the industrial schemes sampled. Industrial occupiers would appear to play a particularly important role in integrating the inner area and national economies.

Finally, as might be expected, Hotel uses appear to attract a relatively small proportion of their customers from the inner area. The majority of customers are relatively equally split between regional and national (UK) markets. However the concentration of competitors within the inner area and region suggests that unless the market for hotel facilities expands to meet the new scheme, the propensity for employment displacement in the inner area will be relatively high.

Indirect Effects: Supply Linkages

Backward supply linkages are the purchases of goods and services from within the inner area which are made by occupiers of assisted schemes. Respondents were asked to identify the proportion of goods and services bought from suppliers in each identified geographical area. Table A2.4 presents the results for our sample.

The inner area is the largest source of suppliers for the sample as a whole. Both the industrial and office schemes in the sample buy the greatest proportion of their goods

Table A2.4 – Location of Suppliers (%)					
Location	Office	Industrial	Retail	Hotel	Sample
Inner Area	45	55	20	38	42
Region	21	15	14	47	23
Rest of UK	30	29	58	15	32
Overseas	4	1	9	0	3
TOTAL	100	100	101	100	100

and services from the inner area. Also notable is the high level of purchasing outside the inner area by retail occupiers. This is explained to a large extent by the fact that many retail occupiers are outlets of national multiples with centralised purchasing and distribution.

In summary it would appear that, where additional to the inner area, industrial and office schemes have the potential to generate backward supply linkages and consequent multiplier effects. Hotel occupiers purchase the highest proportion of their supplies at the regional level although they also generate important supply linkages into the inner area.

Local Income Multiplier: Income Effects

Income effects are, in part, a function of the proportion of additional employees in assisted schemes who are resident in the inner area. They occur where the net income of the inner area population is increased with a resultant increase in the potential for second round expenditure in that area.

Information was gathered from employers on the residency of their employees. This is reproduced in Table A2.5.

These results would suggest that retail schemes offer the greatest potential for creating income multiplier effects in the inner area. Hotel schemes also appear to employ a relatively large proportion of inner area employees whilst both office and industrial schemes draw a much higher proportion of their employees from areas outside the inner area. These percentages refer to all jobs housed in the inner area and not those jobs which are considered additional to the inner area. The proportions are unlikely to be substantially different for net additional jobs.

Table A2.5 – Residency of employees	
Scheme Type	Proportion of Employees in Inner Area (%)
Office	21
Industrial	32
Retail	53
Hotel	46
Sample	34

Printed in the United Kingdom for HMSO
Dd297452 10/93 C10 G531 10170